G.W.F. HEGEL

NATURAL LAW

D0068967

Translated by T.M. KNOX

With an Introduction by H.B. ACTON

Natural Law

Works in Continental Philosophy

General Editor / John R. Silber

G. W. F. Hegel

Natural Law

The Scientific Ways of Treating Natural Law,
Its Place in Moral Philosophy,
and Its Relation to the Positive Sciences of Law

Translated by T. M. Knox
Introduction by H. B. Acton

University of Pennsylvania Press/ 1975

German title: UBER DIE WISSENSCHAFTLICHEN BEHANDLUNGSARTEN DES NATURRECHTS, SEINE STELLE IN DER PRAKTISCHEN PHILOSOPHIE, UND SEIN VERHÄLTNISS ZU DEN POSITIVEN RECHTSWISSENSCHAFTEN

Library of Congress Catalog Card Number: 75-10123

ISBN: 0-8122-7693-0 (cloth)
ISBN: 0-8122-1083-2 (paper)

Manufactured in the United States of America

Editor's Foreword ❧

Perhaps no other philosopher poses greater difficulties for his readers or promises greater rewards for diligent study than Hegel. In writing of the dividends to be derived from the "supreme thought-treasure" of Hegel's works, John N. Findlay has rightly praised Hegel's "stock of invaluable methodological principles by which one's own thought may be guided."

Among these principles is Hegel's concern to preserve the unity of thought and reality, his concern to avoid the bifurcation of the abstract and the concrete, the ideal and the actual. Hegel's thought exemplifies a singleminded concern to avoid what Whitehead later would call "the fallacy of misplaced concreteness." Acutely aware of the philosophical and scientific tendencies to ignore the level of abstraction involved in our description of things, our habit of accepting some reduced and thereby distorted account of the object of thought in lieu of a genuine explanation, Hegel was concerned to comprehend—that is, to transcend a merely manipulative understanding of the world. He was contemptuous of accounts of the world that are merely possible, or that are incomplete and arbitrary descriptions of parts of the world distorted by isolation. He insisted on a philosophical account that could claim to be more than arbitrary, exhaustively concrete, and absolute in its comprehensive interrelatedness.

Nowhere are these central concerns more clearly evidenced in brief scope than in Hegel's essay on *Natural Law*. Appearing at the very beginning of Hegel's prolific philosophical life, this essay provides a useful prologue, both in content and in methodology (which are for Hegel quite inseparable), to what follows. In this early essay are readily apparent Hegel's demonstration of the

5

incompleteness of both formalism and scientific empiricism and his insistence on a pure empiricism and a complete formalism, sustained by concepts that are genuinely absolute. Hegel's intentions stand out in bold relief as he struggles for the movements of thought by which to fulfill them. It is easier, I believe, to understand the full import of Hegel's mature formulations of his basic position when one attends their emergence in this brilliant formative work that, despite its brevity, reveals the comprehensiveness characteristic of Hegel's most extensive writings.

The reader should find substantial assistance in the following introduction by H. B. Acton, which offers a useful commentary on the historical and philosophical background of the *Natural Law* and an exposition and analysis of many of its central issues. In section I, Acton places the *Natural Law* in its immediate historical context and then, in section II, traces Hegel's early philosophical development. In section III, Acton examines Hegel's treatment of natural law within the context of "pure" as opposed to "scientific" empiricism. Hegel's struggle with the formalism of Kant's theory of morality is discussed in section IV, and is followed in section V by a detailed discussion of the relation of the ethical life and the role of law in civil society that distinguishes Hegel's political philosophy from that of Fichte. In section VI, Acton illuminates Hegel's organic view of the ethical life and his conception of the individual as simultaneously a part and a whole of a society. A discussion of Hegel's view of history concludes the introduction.

Acton's introduction should bring the *Natural Law* within the grasp of the beginning student of Hegel while providing a level of scholarship and insight to interest the mature philosopher. This splendid introduction is, lamentably, the last work of Professor Acton, who died soon after its completion.

The translation, by Sir Malcolm Knox, Professor Emeritus of the University of St. Andrews, brings Hegel's ideas faithfully into English. His mastery of Hegel's thought has been indispensable to the success of this translation.

John R. Silber
Boston University

Contents

Introduction ❧

Hegel's essay *The Scientific Ways of Treating Natural Law* appeared in two consecutive parts (December 1802 and May 1803) of the *Kritisches Journal der Philosophie*.[1] This Journal ran from January 1802 until May 1803 and was edited by "Fr. Wilh. Joseph Schelling and Ge. Wilhelm Fr. Hegel" who between them wrote all the contents. The general aims of the *Kritisches Journal* are stated in an announcement of its forthcoming publication in the *Literatur-Zeitung* (December, 1801) and in the Introduction to the first issue entitled "On the Essence of Philosophical Criticism in General, and its Relation to the Present condition of Philosophy in Particular." The announcement refers to "the categorical nature of philosophy," to its "points of contact with the whole of culture" and to "the true rebirth of all sciences through philosophy," while the Introduction expresses hostility to any philosophical claims on behalf of "the healthy human understanding," by relation to which philosophy is said to inhabit "a world in reverse" (*verkehrte Welt*).[2] The "Idea of the Absolute" is presented as rejecting the opposition between idea and reality, between what should be and what is, and the opposition involved in the conception of "an infinite demand." The authors seem not only to be rejecting the philosophy and categories of Common Sense, but also to be hinting at disagreement with Kant and Fichte. Critical Philosophy, as Schelling and Hegel see it, rejects the categories of Common Sense and is no longer satisfied with any "polarity of the inner and the outer" or of "here and beyond." The dualism of Descartes is also attacked and said to be "a dualism in the culture of the modern history of our northwestern world, the decline of a whole mode of aging life, of which the quieter transformations of the public life of men and the noisy revolutions in politics and religion are only variegated manifestations."

At the time when Hegel and Schelling were cooperating in the *Kritisches Journal*, Schelling, although four years younger than Hegel, was much better known. He had published a series of books and articles in support of philosophical idealism, the earliest of which were in the vein of J. G. Fichte, who had made a great stir at Jena until he was accused of atheism and had to leave in 1799. Schelling was also establishing a strange new branch of philosophy, the philosophy of nature, in which experimental physics and chemistry were supplemented by a metaphysical account of natural things and processes. Besides publishing books on this theme, Schelling had edited periodicals about it, written by himself, with the titles *Zeitschrift für spekulative Physik* and the later *Neue Zeitschrift für speckulative Physik*. On Hegel's arrival in Jena, Schelling helped the unknown newcomer to obtain recognition as a lecturer, and Hegel in his turn wrote favorably of Schelling in his first published book *The Difference between the Philosophical Systems of Fichte and Schelling* (1801), known for short as the *Differenzschrift*. J. H. Stirling describes Hegel's philosophical services to Schelling bluntly but amusingly when he says that they were "the *honorarium* or hush money paid by the Unknown to the Known for the privilege of standing on the latter's shoulders and in the light of the latter's fame."[3]

II

Hegel was born at Stuttgart in Württemberg in 1770 and entered the theological college at Tübingen in 1788, the year of publication of Kant's *Critique of Practical Reason*, a book which greatly influenced him. On the outbreak of the French Revolution the next year, Hegel became one of its most vociferous sympathizers at the college. Among his early unpublished writings, written just after his graduation at Tübingen in 1793, are some in which he discusses the nature of a possible religion of the people (*Volksreligion*). This, like the civic religion advocated and to some degree practiced in France during the Revolution, was to spring from the nature and circumstances of the people instead of being received by them from their masters and teachers. It was to be rational, as advocated by

Kant in *Religion Within the Limits of Reason Alone* (1793) and Fichte in *Critique of all Revelation* (1793), which had had the approval of Kant himself. Reason, however, was to work through imagination and myths as it had done in Ancient Greece. Hegel drew a distinction between objective religion, which is its public aspect as expressed in doctrines, dogmas and ceremonies, and subjective religion, which is "a thing of the heart, of concern on account of a need of the practical reason."[4]

From 1793 until 1797 Hegel was a house-tutor at Berne in Switzerland. While he was there he wrote two works which remained unpublished until the twentieth century. The first is a *Life of Jesus* which ends, significantly, with the Crucifixion, and represents Jesus enunciating the Categorical Imperative and recommending an autonomous Kantian morality, although he sometimes refers to "the heart" where Kant would have referred to reason. Another manuscript of the Berne period is *The Positivity of the Christian Religion*. Here, Hegel contrasted the "positive" elements in Christianity, that is, the elements in it which refer to history and revelation and are handed down authoritatively to the believers, with the rational and autonomous religion of Ancient Greece. Jesus, he argued, was unable to secure acceptance for his religion of disinterested rational morality because his disciples, educated in the authoritarian tenets of Judaism, recommended his teachings on his authority instead of on the basis of their inherent rationality. Hegel brings out the contrast by saying that the disciples of Jesus tried to regard the instructions of their Master as authoritative commands, whereas the pupils of Socrates considered themselves his friends and "in their own right they were men as great as Socrates."[5]

At the urgent entreaty of the poet Hölderlin, who had been a fellow student and friend of Hegel at Tübingen, Hegel went to Frankfurt in 1797. His chief work of this period was *The Spirit of Christianity and its Fate*. In it Hegel interprets the teaching of Jesus as a morality of love superior to Kant's morality of law. But according to Hegel a morality of love involves withdrawal from the work and claims of politics and commerce. The unworldly "beautiful soul" who thus emerges—Hegel uses an expression that had been employed by Schiller and Goethe—does not concern himself with the things of Caesar but emulates rather the lilies of the field. Hegel notices that insofar as Jesus was such an unsullied being he inevitably found himself in opposition to the Jewish community, as did his followers afterwards, so that avoiding the world brought them into worldly conflict with it. This "struggle of the pure against the impure," as Hegel called it, is bound to corrupt the pure, so that they become a group of fanatics raging against their fate in a society they cannot evade and cannot alter.[6] Hegel does not mention it, but the *Revelation of St. John* is the work of just such a pure and raging fanatic, and has, indeed, been appealed to by "unwordly" criminal nihilists in our own day.

While Hegel was at Tübingen he was friendly with Schelling, who was a youthful prodigy, and with Hölderlin, who was later to become famous as a poet. Hegel was very closely attached to Hölderlin, to whom he addressed a poem, *Eleusis*, in 1796, and it was at Hölderlin's urgent request and with his help in obtaining a post, that Hegel went to Frankfurt to be near him early the next year. In June or July 1796, while he was still at Berne, Hegel either composed or transcribed an interesting paper which has been given the title "Earliest System-Programme of German Idealism." The authorship was first attributed to Schelling, and the paper is included in Horst Fuhrmans' *F. W. J. Schelling: Briefe und Dokumente*, vol. 1, (Bonn, 1962). It is also included in J. Hoffmeister's *Dokumente zu Hegels Entwickelung* (Stuttgart, 1936), but Hoffmeister does not press Hegel's authorship in his note on the matter. Whoever actually produced the first draft, there can be no doubt that it represents the views of Schelling, Hölderlin and Hegel at the time. It begins by proclaiming the view of Kant's *Critique of Practical Reason* that metaphysics is to be transformed into morality. There are some remarks about the philosophy of nature, but apart from that it is largely concerned with moral and political philosophy regarded as influencing the future of mankind. In March 1796, Fichte's *Foundations of Natural Law* had appeared, and in April of the same year Schelling's *New Deduction of Natural Law* was published in the *Philosophisches Journal*. In part, perhaps, the System-Programme was a response to these, and to Kant's *Perpetual*

Peace which had appeared the previous year.[7] Both Fichte and Schelling had been puzzled by the contrast between morality which, following Kant, they regarded as essentially free and unforced, and legality, which involves the coercion of the recalcitrant. This coercion is carried out by the state, and Hegel (or Hegel-Schelling-Hölderlin) in the System-Programme says that the state is not an Idea, i.e. not "an object of freedom," but a mere mechanism which treats men as "mechanical cogs." Since agreements between states are essential in Kant's *Perpetual Peace*, even this work deals with what is relatively unessential. The important task of the philosopher is to trace the development of freedom, God and immortality in "the history of mankind." Morality or practical reason is basic to free human activity, and if superstition can be overcome, there will emerge "absolute freedom of all spirits which bear the intellectual world in themselves and may not seek for God or immortality *outside themselves*." The author goes on to say that "the philosophy of spirit is an aesthetic philosophy" and that poetry is "the teacher of mankind." The central truths of philosophy, the practical ideas of morality, are to be communicated to the people in the form of myths. Thus philosophy will become mythological and through this the people will become rational. The people will no longer tremble before their sages and priests, and then there will await us "equal development of all powers, of each individual as well as all individuals. No power will be any longer suppressed. Then will reign a universal freedom and equality of all spirits." Hegel's enthusiasm for this hope of social regeneration through the spread of what might be called "practical metaphysics" was expressed by Hegel in a letter to Schelling sent in late January 1795, in which occur the phrases: "let the Kingdom of God come, and let not our hands be idle in our laps," and "Let reason and freedom remain our redemption, and let the invisible church be our point of union."[8]

The superiority of a living popular religion to mere received dogma; the superiority of moral autonomy to a morality of authority and command; the superiority of love to law, but alongside this the recognition that love without law turns into its opposite; the state as a mere mechanism that must be superseded; metaphysics as a response to practical moral demands; freedom as the central feature both of morality and knowledge; the rejection of "the ordinary human understanding," and in particular of dualism; the idea that aesthetic experience reveals reality—these are some of the leading features of Hegel's philosophical outlook before or just after his arrival in Jena in 1801. His first published book, the so-called *Differenzschrift*, appeared that year, and in the early sections of it Hegel set out some of his main views upon the nature and methods of philosophical thinking. Two features of it are of particular importance for our examination of his *Natural Law* essay. The first is that there is a need for philosophy, a need that arises from the existence of unacceptable divisions in our culture and in our thought about it. "Division (*Entzweiung*)," he writes, "is the source of the need for philosophy, and as the culture (*Bildung*) of the age, the unfree given side of the structure. In our culture, that which is an appearance of the Absolute has isolated itself from the Absolute, and determined itself as independent. At the same time, however, the appearance cannot deny its origin, and must therefore proceed to form the multiplicity of its determinations into a whole."[9] Another theme that Hegel develops in this essay concerns Kant's distinction between reason and the understanding. According to Kant's *Critique of Pure Reason* we have to organize our sense experiences in terms of such categories of the understanding as substance and cause in order to obtain objective knowledge of nature, while a constant search for more and more unity in our knowledge helps us to extend it without, however, disclosing objective knowledge of the world as it is in itself. This search for unity is a function, according to Kant, of reason which, therefore, helps practically in the search for knowledge without justifying us in claiming to know how or whether its various departments form a whole. In the *Differenzschrift*, Hegel, while retaining Kant's terminology, rather reverses its import. The understanding, he argues, operates in terms of uncriticized and pre-philosophical categories which it is the business of philosophy to transcend by means of the unifying endeavors of reason. The understanding remains content with a view of the world in terms of things and causes, of immaterial minds and material bodies, of hidden powers and mere appearances. According to Hegel it is the business of philosophy to harmonize these oppositions and divisions in such a way that they cease to be oppositions and divisions but are seen to contribute to a fundamental unity. The philosopher criticizes the divisions of the understanding in the light of the unifying power of reason. In the *Differenzschrift*, Hegel criticises Fichte's moral philosophy for being conducted at the level of the understanding, and for supposing that "disunity and absolute division (*Entzweiung*) constitute the essence of man."[10]

III

The term, "natural law," used by Hegel in the title of this essay, was for many centuries opposed to "positive law," the law that force, accident and particular deliberation have brought into existence in the various countries of the world. Natural law, on the other hand, consisted of fundamental rational principles of public behavior, the same everywhere and always, which ought and often do guide legislators in framing the laws of particular states. By the eighteenth century the doctrine of natural law had engendered the doctrine of natural rights, rights that the legislation of all countries ought to respect and maintain. The American and French Revolutions gave practical reinforcement to the idea that it is irrational and unacceptable for governments arbitrarily to deprive individuals of their freedom or their property. Human society was regarded as coming into being by the association of individuals who might have chosen to live in scattered isolation, and once a society had been formed, the members of it could proceed to set up or submit to some form of government. Individuals entered into contracts in order to pass from what was called a state of nature to what was called civil society. The state of nature had no law except the natural law, while civil society—called by Hegel "the state of law" (*Rechtszustand*)—had a government which makes and applies positive law. Variations on this general pattern of law and society are to be found in the writings of such philosophers as Locke, Hobbes, Spinoza, Pufendorf, and Rousseau, and in eighteenth century Germany, books and articles on the subject generally had the word *Naturrecht*, "natural law," in the title. By Hegel's time, indeed, the expression was coming to mean what today we should call general jurisprudence or the philosophy of law. Even so, Hegel's use of it in the title of this essay is somewhat paradoxical, since he rejects the whole idea that society is deliberately formed by the association of pre-existing individuals. Indeed, he goes further than this and in effect holds that the positive law of each state is more rational and fundamental than any supposed law of nature held to be valid always and everywhere. In 1821 he gave "Natural Law and Political Science in Outline" as an alternative title to his *Elements of the Philosophy of Right*, and as late as 1866 Hegel's follower, Carl Michelet, called his book on the philosophy of society, *Natural Law or the Philosophy of Right*.[11]

Schelling and Hegel both regarded themselves as heirs of Kant's so-called Critical Philosophy or, as Schelling called it, Transcendental Idealism. Nowadays there is a tendency on the part of philosophers who support Empiricism to consider Kant's *Critique of Pure Reason* as a work of destruction, as a refutation of transcendent metaphysics, and as a defense of an agnostic form of positivism. Kant, these philosophers supposed, showed the impossibility of proving the existence of God and the immortality of the soul, showed too that the empirical sciences must be based on observation and experiment free from metaphysical considerations, and showed finally that morality must be freed from dogmatic religion. Schelling and Hegel, however, thought that Kant had opened the way for something much more positive than this. We have seen how Hegel transformed Kant's distinction between reason and the understanding into a distinction between naive and dispersed thinking on the one hand, and self-conscious and unified thinking on the other, that is, between empirical science and philosophy. We have seen, too, that Hegel and Schelling regarded Kant's reinstatement of God, freedom, and immortality as Postulates of *Practical* reason as the reinstatement of metaphysics itself in a new form. Morality is better able than logical argument, they thought, to lead us from the merely relative and incomplete (the sphere of the understanding) to the absolute whole (the object of the reason). Later they came to believe that art and religion can do this better than morality. At the beginning of the *Natural Law* essay, therefore, Hegel regrets that

Kant and his followers, having shown that the various empirical sciences are concerned with appearances and what is merely relative and are hence distinct from philosophy, have not been able to recover them for philosophy (p. 57). According to Hegel it is the task of philosophy to establish the positive contribution of each empirical science and to define its differences from and relation to the rest. In the case of the science of natural law, he says, this means that it must be related to "the ethical, the mover of all things human" (p. 58). This may seem obvious, but Hegel has in mind the view, which may be regarded as an exaggeration of Kant's account of the relation of law to morality, that since morality is the sphere of conscience, freedom and autonomy, while positive law is the sphere of enforcement and coercion, law can in no way be derived from morality. Schelling had wrestled with this problem in his *New Deduction of Natural Law*, where he argued that coercing someone is treating him as a mere natural object so that the very activity of enforcing natural law destroys it, turning it into a process in the natural world. Coercion and enforcement belong to the world of nature, not to the world of freedom, which is the world of morality.[12] As we shall see, Fichte in his *Foundation of Natural Law* (1796-7) drew the conclusion that law and morality are quite distinct, and when, therefore, Hegel says that the science of natural law must be related to the ethical he is consciously going against Fichte's view. He is also anticipating his later argument that coercion is in a sense impossible among rational beings and that morality and law are continuous and inseparable.

Hegel considered that there had hitherto been two principal ways of treating the science of natural law and that both of them are faulty. The one way is predominantly empirical, the other purely formal and *a priori*. The empirical treatment has two main forms. On the one hand there are relatively untheoretical descriptive accounts of existing legal institutions, and on the other hand there are attempts to explain particular institutions or the origins and nature of civil society in terms of some single empirically observable factor or faculty. The institution of marriage, for example, may be explained in terms of the single basic factor of procreation, and punishment in terms of reform or deterrence (p. 60). Again, in order to explain the transition from the state of nature to the state of law (civil society) the individuals supposed to exist in the state of nature are provided with characteristics and desires which make the transition appear necessary. The individuals, for example, are said to possess a gregarious instinct, or the strong are said to have subdued the weak (p. 65).

With his eye on the logical similarities between the two theories, Hegel compares the theory of a state of nature from which civil society emerges with the theory of an original chaos from which the ordered physical world has developed (p. 63). The concept of a chaotic state of nature, he argues, is reached by a process of abstracting from what is said to be particular and merely accidental in an actual civil society or state of law. The factors and faculties present in the state of nature must be selected, he holds, so as to make it possible to derive from them the faculties of civilized men and the factors that make up civil society. This, he goes on, is a surreptitious derivation of what was intended to be *a priori* from what is in fact *a posteriori*; that is, the derivation of civil society from the state of nature is not, as it is made to appear, the derivation of what is secondary from what is basic and primary. It is rather the arbitrary attribution to the state of nature of those characteristics from which civil society can be derived (p. 64). Furthermore, this empiricist way of treating the science of natural law, involving as it does the arbitrary selection of some single characteristic or function as basic—say, self-preservation (as by Hobbes) or deterrence as the essence of punishment (as by utilitarians)—soon shows its one-sided inadequacy and will be opposed by other characteristics or functions, i.e., by sociability as the basis of civil society or by reform as the essence of punishment.

Hegel now goes on to contrast the sort of empiricism we have so far considered, called by him "scientific empiricism" (p. 67), with the purely descriptive empiricism which attempts to provide a total, untheoretical "picture" or "intuition" of society or of some institution, which he calls "pure empiricism" (p. 62, p. 67). Scientific empiricism obtains its form of unity by abstracting a single quality which is said to characterize every individual. Pure empiricism provides a pictorial view of the whole in all its variety and complexity. It may be naive but it is not deliberately one-sided. We come nearer, for example, to a philosophical view of punishment if we are told by a non-philosophical or unpretentious observer that it has in it elements of "revenge, security of the state, reform, execution of a threat, deterrence, prevention, etc." (p. 69), than if these different facets are separated from one another, or one of them is emphasized at the expense of the rest. Complexity may engender a certain amount of confusion, but naively complex confusion is less misleading than simplified abstraction. The logical basis of unity in the "scientific" empiricist's procedure is the single characteristic or factor taken as basic. The choice is arbitrary, the unity therefore imposed rather than native, and the whole is in consequence incompletely organized.

It is obvious that a theory about the nature of philosophy in general and about the status of empiricism is implicit in all this. Since his arrival in Jena in 1801, Hegel had given lectures not only on natural law but also on logic and metaphysics.[13] Karl Rosenkranz quotes from Hegel's programmatic introduction to his lectures on logic and metaphysics to the effect that he was proposing to begin his lectures on logic with an account of our knowledge of the finite, and then to pass on to a discussion of philosophical knowledge, which is knowledge of the infinite.[14] From this and from the *Jena Logic* of 1804–5 we discover that the realm of the finite is dominated by the categories of the understanding and is the world of distinct and simple qualities, of separate units and aggregations of them, and of a false sort of infinity which consists in the indefinite endless repetition of the same.[15] The qualities and individuals in this world are each of them self-contained, and are related to one another by the undemanding connectedness of "and."[16] The individuals have this, that, and the other distinct quality, and each individual is separated from the others by definite boundaries.

What is the connection of this ticketed, numbered and repetitious world with the philosophy of empiricism? Hegel saw it as the logical framework of the view that knowledge is basically sensation; that, as Destutt de Tracy was at this very time saying in France, "*penser, c'est sentir.*" We may compare it, too, with Bacon's view of knowledge as concerned ultimately with "simple natures" which are the alphabet out of which the complexities of nature are formed. Sense experience is inadequate not because it is "derived from the senses," but because it is supposed to be made up from simple, self-identical, disjoined and repetitious units. What is wrong with empiricism is its metaphysics, which is the metaphysics of the finite. The finite reaches a higher level when the individuals are not indifferent to one another as they are at the level of mere sensation. Causes and their effects and interacting substances are in this closer relationship of interdependence, to which Hegel gives the name "*Verhältniss.*" The terms of a "*Verhältniss,*" Hegel writes, "only have meaning in connection with one another . . .";[17] and he says that in the practical sciences such as natural law we are concerned not with "pure qualities, but relations" (*Verhältnisse*) (p. 58). Such concepts as self-preservation, or love and hate, essentially involve two or more terms.

The idea of a logic or metaphysics of empiricism may seem strange, but Hegel made it an important element in his system. A further account of it is given in his *Phenomenology of Mind* (1807) in the discussion of "sense certainty," and the logic and metaphysics of it is developed in his *Science of Logic* (1812) in the section headed "The Doctrine of Being." The general idea is that the empiricist takes things as they are and regards each element of experience in isolation from the rest. Yet the very boundaries and limitations of the basic qualities of being introduce intimations of relationships beyond them, so that the qualities are no longer accepted at their face value or just as they seem. Simple being then gives way to essence, sheer immediacy to the contrast between how things seem and how they are, between forces exercised and mere potentialities. Already in the *Natural Law* essay this scheme is adumbrated in the distinction between "pure qualities" and "relations" (p. 58). It has been suggested, indeed, that Kant himself did not regard sensibility as an original fact merely to be accepted as such, but rather as a consequence of man's limitations and finitude in the spheres of both knowledge and action.[18]

In his account of "scientific empiricism" Hegel says that some single quality or function such as self-preservation or deterrence is selected from a complex social whole and held to be the prime moving force in it. But the selection is arbitrary and cannot do justice to the complex unity of the whole. In consequence, self-preservation, say, is opposed by sympathy, or deterrence by reform, and the result is an impasse. These different "qualities," says Hegel, "cancel each other out and are reduced to nullity" (p. 65). This, it would seem, is a rather rough account of how illegitimate abstraction sets the dialectical method in motion, although Hegel did not make much use of it until later.

IV

Having rejected the empiricist way of explaining human society and institutions, Hegel turns to what he calls "Formalism." He has in mind Kant's ethical theory and Fichte's *Foundation of Natural Law* (1796–7).

This is not the place to describe Kant's moral philosophy in any detail, but the reader may be reminded that, in distinguishing between the form and the matter of our moral principles, Kant argued that only those maxims of conduct are morally acceptable which can be acted on or willed without contradiction by all rational beings. The moral law, he held, is *a priori* and rational, a deliverance of the rational will or practical reason. A purely rational being would conform to the moral law with no sense of constraint or obligation because, being devoid of contrary desires or inclinations, he would have nothing within him to hold him back from such conformity. Human beings, however, possess desires and inclinations as well as reason, and their desires to satisfy and advantage themselves come into conflict with the universal, rational moral law, and give rise to the concept and the consciousness of obligation or duty, the consciousness of being forced or commanded through the moral law. The conflicts between one's own personal happiness and the general good, between inclination and duty are, according to Kant, a central feature of morality. Since there can be no duty to do what one cannot do, morality presupposes freedom to act, and freedom is the power of the rational to overcome the sensible attractions of individual desire. A consistently successful selfish man must have his desires under control and is therefore rational, but his reason is at the service of his self-interest; his choices are particular and personal, whereas moral choices are universal and impersonal. According to Kant moral reason is not subservient to personal ends. In morality, morality is the end, and the practice of it is itself rational, whereas the rationality of choosing the means to happiness depends on the theoretical knowledge of natural causes. The demand or imperative of practical reason is absolute, categorical and applicable always, everywhere and to everyone.

This account of morality is manifestly not empirical. An empiricist such as Hume must take human desires as he finds them and regard morality as a strategy for their satisfaction with the least frustration possible. In consequence, rules of behavior become matters of utility for the empiricist and must vary according to time, place and circumstance. If, as Hume believed, there is some trace of benevolence in everyone, the rule of beneficence may be universal, but it is a matter of degree and there is nothing absolute or categorical about it, and Hume may be wrong or some natural occurrence may extinguish benevolence from the world. But as seen by Kant, morality is not contingent, and is not localized or a matter of degree. It is universal and unalterable. Kant's formalism consists in abstracting from the historically and geographically contingent so as to obtain a principle that is cosmopolitan and eternal. The whole of history, past, present and future, is within its ambit and subject to its judgment.

In his *Life of Hegel* (1844), Rosenkranz says that there existed at that time a commentary written by Hegel in 1798 on Kant's *Metaphysic of Morals* which had been published the previous year. From what Rosenkranz says, it appears that Hegel attempted to unite the two parts of the *Metaphysic of Morals*, Part I, the *Metaphysical Elements of Justice*, and Part II, the *Metaphysical Elements of Virtue*, into a single whole which would combine "the legality of positive law and the morality (*Moralität*) of the inward consciousness of one's own goodness or badness." In this commentary Hegel called this unity "life"—later he called it "ethical life" (*Sittlichkeit*). According to Rosenkranz, Hegel also "protested against the suppression of nature by Kant and the dismemberment of man brought about by a casuistry that is dominated by the concept of duty." Hegel also objected to Kant's belief that Church and State can exist side by side without encroaching on one another. "If man as a whole," he wrote, "is shattered into a citizen and a member of the Church, the living whole of the Church becomes a mere fragment." In the next pages of the *Life*, Rosenkranz quotes from another manuscript of the time which is relevant to the *Natural Law* essay. In it Hegel is considering what Rosenkranz calls "the present world-crisis," and says that although there is no longer any liking for "the sycophantic little world" of the *ancien régime*, it cannot be overcome by a force from outside, as this would be one particular against another particular rather than the growth of a new unity. As to Germany, its constitution is only a mere thought and there is no longer a sovereign power. This has been decided by public opinion through a loss of trust or confidence (*Zutrauen*). We shall see later that one of Hegel's objections to Fichte's account of positive law is that in it law and the state were supposed to be independent of "faith and constancy" (p. 84 below), and that force was held to be more effective than it can be. "Coercion," Hegel writes, "is nothing real, nothing in itself . . ." (p. 88).[19]

Although Hegel, as we have seen, had studied Kant's philosophy of law, what he criticizes in the *Natural Law* essay is his moral philosophy, and this as. presented in the *Critique of Practical Reason*. For his fundamental statement of Kant's formalism he gives the following: "[so act] that a maxim of thy will shall count at the same time as a principle of universal legislation" (p. 76 below, quoted from the *Critique of Practical Reason*, Book I, ch. 1, §7.). It is not without significance that Hegel has omitted the word "always" (*jederzeit*), which in Kant's text occurs immediately before "at the same time." The omission is obviously inadvertent, since inclusion of the word would have sharpened Hegel's historical account of morality in contrast with Kant's view of it as eternal as well as universal. Nevertheless it does suggest an unconscious refusal on Hegel's part to go along with Kant in the use of "*jederzeit*" with its implication of moral principles which transcend history. We shall see that although Hegel continues to use the Kantian terminology about "the universal," he changes its meaning.

Hegel's first criticism of Kant's formula of universal legislation is interesting and fundamental. He points out that in the *Critique of Pure Reason* Kant had argued that the purely formal principles of logic, which amount to non-contradiction or self-consistency, cannot determine whether a proposition is true or not, since truth is correspondence with an object, and, from the fact that a proposition is not self-contradictory, nothing can be concluded about its correspondence or non-correspondence with fact. Considerations of content or matter must be taken into account over and above the formal consideration of mere consistency if we are to know whether or not a proposition is true. It is Hegel's argument that Kant forgets all this when he sets out his theory of morality and argues that "the will . . . . is thought of as determined by the mere form of the moral law. . ." (*Critique of Practical Reason*, Book I, ch. i, §7). Such formalism, Hegel continues, is really a principle of *immorality*, since all sorts of rules of wickedness could be adopted and justified on the ground that they are not self-contradictory—". . . in this way," he writes, "anything specific can be made into a duty" (p. 79). Kant had supported his case with the example of a man who, knowing he cannot be found out, keeps a deposit that had been left with him without a receipt. This, Kant says, could not be done by everyone, since if everyone were to try to do it, no one would ever entrust any property to anyone else, and there would be no more deposits. Hegel's objection is that there is no contradiction in there not being any deposits, but only between there being deposits and there not being deposits. He generalizes this and says that deposits presuppose property and that Kant is in effect saying that the cheat in his example is going against the institution of property, and this amounts to saying that, "property is property and nothing else. And this tautological production is the legislation of this practical reason; property, if property *is*, must be property" (p. 78). Hegel repeated this objection in 1821 in §135 of the *Philosophy of Right*, and Professor W. H. Walsh in discussing it in his *Hegelian Ethics* (1969) says the objection could equally be used about Kant's famous argument in the *Groundwork of the Metaphysic of Morals*, that if everyone broke their promises, "promising and the very purpose of promising" would become impossible. Walsh suggests that this shows that you cannot both "accept the institution of promise-keeping and repudiate something which necessarily goes with it," but goes on to say that it does not follow "that a world without promises would be morally inferior to the existing world." [20]

In the first place we may notice that although, according to Kant, a maxim of action which would lead to contradiction if universalized must be rejected as wrong, he does not say that the formal principle of non-contradiction is the principle of morality. For the procedure of universalizing cannot be carried out except by reference to a maxim which has a content. The common objection, therefore, that Kant's categorical imperative is an "empty formalism" is quite misleading, as Professor Marcus Singer has shown in his *Generalisation in Ethics*.[21] But Singer goes too far when he says that Hegel's criticism is "almost incredibly simple-minded," for Hegel had two important problems in mind when he was criticizing Kant which cannot be brushed aside as trivial.

The first of these concerns the form and matter of practical judgments. The distinction between form and matter, Hegel held, is linked with the distinction between reason and sensibility, and is concerned also with the distinction between different types of unity. We have already seen that, according to Hegel, a human society cannot consist of a plurality of individuals all of whom possess some single characteristic or aim. A society must have a closer and more complex unity than that of a class in the logical sense. Hegel thought that Kant's idea of a Kingdom of Ends composed of free, rational beings was too much like this. Furthermore, Kant sharply distinguished reason from sense and regarded reason as something from another world intervening in the sensible world to bring order into it. At the social level, the rational will would act through a divine legislator to bring a horde of human animals under control, and at the level of the individual man the rational will has the task of subduing the passions and desires. Hegel believed, however, that form and matter, reason and sensibility, the one and the many are much more closely connected than this in the human sphere, and as we proceed we shall see in more detail how he thought this was possible.

This carries implications for Hegel's view of practical reason, for Kant's practical reason, he believed, is just such an external rational will. Rationality, according to Hegel, is more than logical consistency, and is exhibited by each individual through the unity of his life rather than by the mere logical consistency of the maxims he adopts. Reason shows itself in society through "the spirit" of its laws and policies rather than in any single aim pursued by all its members. If Hegel had discussed Kant's *Groundwork* with its example of lying promises which cannot be made by everyone, instead of the *Critique of Practical Reason* with the example of the deposit, he might have shown more sympathy for Kant's conception of the categorical imperative. For the trust involved in promising appears to be essential to any persisting human society. Could there be anything rational, in a practical way, about a human society in which it was not worth while to make promises, or in which truthfulness counted for nothing?

Hegel also criticizes Kant's categorical imperative of universal legislation by bringing forward examples of moral rules which cannot be accommodated to it. The first of these is the maxim "help the poor" which, he says, "elevated into a principle of universal legislation, will prove to be false because it annihilates itself" (p. 80). Hegel's argument seems to be that if the maxim is carried out successfully, there will be no poor left to help or the rich will ruin themselves and everyone will be poor with no one left to help them, and if the poor are kept in being so that the maxim may be acted on, the maxim is not really being acted on. A few years later in the *Phenomenology of Mind* Hegel developed this to the point of arguing that morality as conceived of by Kant is always in danger of succeeding and of abolishing itself by its very success. Indeed, he goes further than this and suggests that there is inevitably something shifty about it because of this feature of it which we cannot help recognizing and yet feel we must exclude from our consciousness.[22] In the *Philosophy of Right*, however, he says that there will always be plenty for morality (*Moralität*, i.e., morality as Kant saw it) to do in relieving poverty by means of private help, but public help becomes necessary in modern societies and may take the form of discovering and finding remedies for the general conditions which make some people poor (§242). Thus Hegel later relaxed his thesis of the paradox of morality in the light of his later reflections on the nature of poverty in modern societies, and came to recognize that private charity can exist alongside public provision. Nevertheless, the paradox of morality was intended by Hegel to cast doubt on the absoluteness of the Kantian morality of self-imposed universal law and, by virtue of its incoherence, to justify acceptance of the community-oriented morality of "ethical life" (*Sittlichkeit*). The second maxim which he thinks cannot be accomodated to the principle of universal legislation, that of "honorably defending one's country against its enemies" (p. 80), illustrates this more directly.

Hegel's argument that the universal legislation principle cannot be accommodated to the maxim of honorably defending one's country against its enemies is not stated in detail. His words are that if it is universalized, "the specification of country, enemies and defence is cancelled" (p. 80). This seems to mean that when universalized, the maxim becomes the principle: "Everyone ought always to defend his country honorably against its enemies," and in consequence it is not only about one's own country, but about countries generally and about defenders and enemies generally. In reply to this it could be argued that the particular contents of *any* maxim *must* become general when universalized because of the very meaning of the word. It is wrong for me to deceive my particularly close friend, but this is not denied, it may be said, when it is shown that there is a contradiction in the concept of all particularly close friends deceiving one another. But am I not defending something different when I defend my country from what others defend when they defend theirs? Hegel's point, I think, is that each country is unique and that the individual's loyalty is to it rather than to some principle about patriotism generally. To this the Kantian may reply that however much the details are specified, we can and should always ask whether the action in these circumstances could be carried out by everyone who found himself in them, or whether or not this very specifically determined type of country with such and such a specific type of enemy could be honorably defended. It might, for example, be thoroughly corrupt, and its enemies may have justice on their side. Hegel seems to be saying that loyalty to one's country is not like subscribing to principles of honesty or benevolence involving the universal repetition of similar conduct in similar circumstances. By patriotism the individual is attached to those particular men who form this particular society rather than to all patriots everywhere.[23] The society is a whole, not a class, and each member is a part rather than an instance.[24]

V

On p. 17 above mention was made of Schelling's article on Natural
Law, in which he pointed out the problem which arises when force,
even legal force, is exercized over free individuals. To force or
coerce anyone, Schelling argued, is to treat him as if he were a mere
physical object, and hence to act on him as if he were nothing but a
part of the physical world. This essay appeared in 1796 about the
same time as Fichte's *Foundations of Natural Law*, in which the
same problem receives much more extensive treatment. It should be
noticed that Fichte's book appeared before *Kant's Metaphysics of
Morals* (1797) in which, in the part headed *Metaphysical Elements
of Justice*, Kant had presented his philosophy of law. This shows
that the conventional way of writing the history of philosophy, in
which the views of each famous philosopher are presented as a
continuous whole and each philosopher is discussed after his
"predecessors" and before his "successors," can be seriously
misleading. Although Fichte, Schelling and Hegel are all regarded as
"successors" of Kant, each of them wrote works of significance
during Kant's lifetime in which they considered themselves
developing views they had obtained from him. They each published
on the philosophy of law before Kant himself (if we except
Perpetual Peace[1795], which Fichte discusses in a long footnote),
and from what they regarded as a Kantian point of view, and it is
possible that Kant read their views on law, or views similar to them,
before he published his *Metaphysics of Morals*. The history of
philosophy, as distinct from the history of philosophers, is a history
of books, articles and arguments rather than of intellectual careers.
In such a history the lives and careers of individual philosophers
would be subordinated to the impersoanl intellectual world of
books, articles and reviews.

Fichte's *Foundations of Natural Law* is a work of very
considerable analytic power. The starting point is a world of
independent and free individuals each with a body which is subject
to the laws of physical nature. Human action is inconceivable except
in such a world. Acting involves affecting things and bodies in space
and time which are subject to natural necessity, yet morality is a

matter of intention, good will and freedom. How then is this subjective moral law related to legality, the objective positive law with its rules about injuries to human bodies and the removal or recovery of material property? The purpose of association in society, according to Fichte, is to enable each and every free individual to have a sphere for the exercise of his freedom. This can be achieved only insofar as each individual limits the sphere of his free activities to the extent that this is necessary to enable others to act freely as well. This cannot, however, be left to the conscience of each individual, for people do violate one another's rights, and it is impossible to look into the mind of another and read there the sincerity of his promises. Even if one could, misunderstandings and mistakes are possible. The commands of morality are categorical, allowing nothing to the wishes of the individual, but laws that uphold rights are permissive and need not be appealed to by the injured party; sometimes, indeed, it would be wrong for an individual to stand on his rights, and if law were derived from morality this could not be possible. Again, positive law calls for obedience irrespective of the motive, but the moral law must be followed for its own sake if the individual's action is to be morally good. Fichte goes so far as to say that the sphere of legality "has nothing to do with the moral law." [25]

For civil society to come into existence, the argument proceeds, the would-be members of it must reciprocally recognize one another as free agents and devise a mechanism for their mutual security. One individual cannot obtain security without the others having it too, but "faith and constancy," [26] although morally desirable, are not what is required here since no one can be sure that others, or even themselves when the time for action comes, will keep faith and remain constant. Guarantees can only be obtained if a third party, rather like Hobbes's sovereign, will keep the individuals in their proper spheres and they can be sure that he will do this. When an individual violates the rights of another he does so in order to obtain something that he wants. If, however, he is sure that by violating the rights of another he will not get what he wants but something he emphatically does not want, he will keep within his sphere and not invade the spheres of others. He does this, not as a purely rational being, but nevertheless as a partially rational being, and as rational he *need* not submit to the threat of the law, but "can resist and overcome every force of nature."[27] But a well established police and legal system would ensure the apprehension and punishment of lawbreakers with what would be "mechanical and natural power"[28] or "mechanical necessity"[29] if such were possible among free individuals. These, however, in becoming free, have risen above the purely natural.

There is no space here to describe Fichte's defense of the social contract and his development of Rousseau's theory of the General Will. Since Hegel refers to it, however, Fichte's idea for a new type of office, the "ephorate," should be noticed. Everyone recognizes that, even in a well-ordered state, the executive has the power to interfere with the working of the constitution, and may even pervert or destroy it. Convinced that the legal aspects of society must work without "faith and constancy,"[30] Fichte tries to invent a device which would *make* the executive confine itself to its proper functions. The result is the ephorate, a body which it would be high treason to intimidate, entrusted with the power to call the executive to account if it appears to be overstepping its constitutional powers. The ephorate would have the duty to suspend or abolish the legal powers of the executive and to call upon the whole people to meet together to deal with the emergency, and Fichte thought that its ability to coerce the executive would be ensured by the fact that it could pronounce that its members were henceforth to be regarded as merely private persons. Such an institution would be an essential element in what Fichte calls a rational state (*Vernunftstaat*).

Given Hegel's view that it is the business of philosophy to overcome division (*Entzweiung*), it is only to be expected that he would oppose Fichte's sharp division between legality and morality. In the *Differenzschrift*(1801), the work in which he had emphasized the philosophical importance of overcoming division, Hegel devoted some very trenchant paragraphs to Fichte's views on natural law. Fichte's state, Hegel asserted, is not, as Fichte claimed, a rational state (*Vernunftstaat*), but a state at the level of the understanding (*Verstandes-Staat*)—"a building," Hegel writes, "in which reason has no part; reason therefore rejects it because it must find itself most expressively in the most complete system of organs and functions (*Organisation*) that it can give itself, in forming itself into a people (*in der Selbstgestaltung zu einem Volk*). But [Fichte's] state at the level of the understanding is not a system of organs and functions but a machine; the people [as he describes it] is not the organic body of a rich and common life, but an atomistic, lifeless plurality, the elements of which are absolutely opposed substances . . . *Fiat justitia pereat mundus* is the law of this state, not in the sense in which Kant asserted it—let the right be done even if all the rogues in the world perish—but: the right must be done even though in consequence trust, pleasure and love, all the capacities of a genuinely moral identity were to be extirpated."[31] In the *Natural Law* essay, Hegel says that Fichte's state at the level of the understanding "really is an attempt at a consistent system which would have no need of the religion and ethics that are foreign to it" (p. 85). It is at this point that Hegel claims to characterize Fichte's position by borrowing from him the phrase "arrangement working with mechanical necessity."

It is interesting to compare Hegel's assessment of Fichte's analysis of positive law and the state with that of a twentieth century writer. Xavier Léon in his *Fichte et son Temps* (Paris, 1922) says that Fichte's social pact "makes of the multiplicity of the individuals, independent if not in rivalry with one another, an organic whole, a Society," and goes on to say that Fichte "regards the isolated individual as a single entity, an empty concept, and only confers on him value and reality when he is a member of the social community" (p. 499). Hegel's view is that the unity of Fichte's wrongly named "rational state" rests on force rather than on reason and is mechanical rather than organic. The difference could hardly be greater.

But Hegel uses the quotation from §14 of Fichte's *Naturrecht* in a misleading way. Fichte's actual words are: "If in consequence an arrangement working with mechanical necessity could be hit upon . . . ," and earlier in the same section he had written: "No arrangement can or should be hit upon according to which actions which should not happen would be prevented by mechanical natural power; this is in part impossible, because man is free, and for this very reason can resist and overcome every force of nature; and in part it is contrary to the nature of law, because by such an arrangement man, in the field of legal concepts, would be made into a mere machine, and the freedom of his will would count for nothing. The arrangement to be hit upon would thus have to direct itself to the will itself and enable and oblige it to determine itself by its own power to will nothing except what can be consistent with freedom under the law."[32] Unlike Schelling in his *System of Transcendental Idealism* (see Note 23), Fichte in this passage does not regard men as merely reacting to pain or uneasiness, but as rationally directing their actions and realizing that their aims will be frustrated if they break the law of their country. Hegel was wrong, therefore, to reproach Fichte with having a mechanical conception of the state and with supposing that free men can be coerced as if they were nothing but natural objects.

However, Fichte's misnamed "rational state" is a device set up by a plurality of free individuals in order to obtain security and opportunities to pursue their personal aims. This arrangement, according to Fichte, is not a matter of conscience or loyalty. He actually uses the word *Rechtshandel* for legal disputes within this system, and the reader cannot fail to think of cattle dealing (*Kuhhandel*) and of trade generally. "Legal dealing," as we may translate *Rechtshandel*, is treated by Fichte as if it were a sort of trading or bargaining. The state, as he sees it, exists in that unsentimental arena where wary dealers squeeze the utmost out of one another. In the *Nicomachean Ethics*[33] Aristotle mentions that there was a statue to the Graces in the market at Athens, and I think he means that even trade requires some species of friendship between those who take part in it. Certainly Hegel did not believe that a state could be formed by a contract between Fichte's amoral libertarians. He goes on to argue that free men cannot be coerced (*gezwungen*) but can be subdued or overcome (*bezwungen*) (p. 90). Threats cannot make a free man do what the utterer of them wants him to do, since the free man can accept the penalty rather than do what he is being required to do. In the last resort he can die rather than submit and so the victory is his: "By his ability to die the subject proves himself free and entirely above all coercion. Death is the absolute subjugator (*die absolute Bezwingung*)" (p. 91).

This is not meant as rhetoric, but as an attempt to give a more adequate account of freedom than Fichte's description of it as distributed in limited stocks among individuals who want to keep all others from their limited spheres. As Hegel sees it, Fichte subordinates freedom to security instead of treating it as absolute. Death would destroy the security and "empirical freedom" (p. 90) which Fichte's "rational state" is intended to maintain. If freedom is an absolute it cannot be a means to something else and cannot be described in terms of the finite categories of the understanding. If it lifts men above physical nature it must be characterized in quite different terms. Fichte, by regarding it as limited and shared out, considers it at the wrong level, as if it were subject to the categories of "relation" (p. 20 above).

These considerations, Hegel thought, also have their relevance to the institution of punishment. If the state were like Fichte's picture of it and law were to be regarded as upheld by threats intended to outweigh the benefits anticipated by breaking it, punishments would be like elements in a commercial deal. The law-enforcing body would have crimes on offer to those who, as we say, were willing to pay the penalties (p. 92). But this again is looking at the matter in terms of quite the wrong categories. It should be remembered that when Hegel was writing this essay almost all crimes were punishable with death, so that it was natural for him to relate the two. In so far as the criminal deliberately risks his life he is acting as a free man, so that liability to punishment by death and freedom go together, and when he is hanged he is subdued and overcome but not coerced. If punishment were deterrence or treatment, it would consist of a manipulation of men's passions and desires in the service of ulterior ends. Insofar as freedom is central in it, it is as absolute as freedom is.

Hegel also says that "retribution alone is rational" in punishment (p. 92), and appears to give a schematic description of what retribution is when he says that, the "state of affairs $+A$, brought about by the crime, is complemented (*ergänzt*) [we might also translate *ergänzt* by "completed"] by the bringing about of $-A$, and so both are annihilated" (p. 92). It is unfortunate that although he uses the symbols $+A$ and $-A$ several times, and even says (p. 90) that +A −A = 0, Hegel never says precisely what they stand for, and never gives examples. In the case of punishment, however, it seems reasonable to suppose that "+A" stands for the crime, say the murder of a man, and "−A" for the punishment, say the execution of the murderer. This seems to be a scheme of what we ordinarily mean by retribution, but how does the execution complement or complete the murder? I do not think we need to speculate about this or to look for hints in Hegel's later writings. About the same time as he was writing the *Natural Law* essay, he also wrote an account of "moral life," the so-called *System der Sittlichkeit*, which was not published until after his death. In spite of its obscurities—Hegel often uses Schelling's philosophical terminology without explaining it—it can be used as a sort of commentary on parts of the *Natural Law* essay, and it does contain a more explicit account of punishment. When a crime is committed, Hegel here says, a real injury is done to the victim. The wrong-doer who has inflicted this real injury becomes conscious of a bad conscience and suffers from remorse. Remorse, however, is abstract, ideal and subjective, whereas if it were a concrete reality it would have to be both ideal and real and both subjective and objective. The wrong-doer's conscience, therefore, confronts the crime with only ideal "opposition" (*Gegenwirkung*) and "reversal" (*Umkehrung*), and "avenging justice" remedies these "imperfections." "The consciousness of his own annihilation (*Vernichtung*)," Hegel writes, "is subjective, internal, a bad conscience. To this extent it is incomplete, and must show itself externally as avenging justice. Because it is internal and imperfect, it impels towards totality. It betrays, reveals and labors within itself until it sees the ideal opposition and reversal standing over against it and threatening its reality from outside. Then it tries to find relief for itself, because it sees the beginning of its reality in this enemy."[34]

This shows that Hegel's scheme of +A and −A is not detailed enough. He is saying, rather, that when a free man commits a crime his conscience will trouble him and he will feel remorse. But he will also feel that the ideal, internal, self-inflicted vengeance that constitutes this remorse is inadequate in the face of a crime that was real and external. This inadequacy or imperfection calls for a real and external vengeance to complete it. A man who commits a crime and feels remorse for it cannot remain satisfied with making this merely subjective response. His internal tears are crocodile tears unless he is ready to face an avenger who makes him shed real ones. Hegel's analysis of the institution of punishment here and in the *System der Sittlichkeit* illustrates his view that morality in a categorical and finally acceptable form must be a matter of outward deeds as well as of internal intentions. If actions are to be real and objective they must also make their place in a system of social institutions. But if ideal intentions are abstracted from real actions, "ethical life" (*Sittlichkeit*) becomes mere conscientiousness (*Moralität*—see p. 112 with Knox's note) and this only too easily gets perverted into an idle and shifty shadow of morality.[35]

In the *Differenzschrift* Hegel had said that Fichte's detailed proposals for the constitution of his "rational state," and particularly the institution of the ephorate, were likely to lead in practice to a large amount of harassing legislation with the professed aim of protecting each individual's freedom. In the *Natural Law* essay he goes into more detail (p. 87, p. 121). He doubts, for example, whether the existence of an ephorate would have prevented Napoleon from taking control of the state in his Brumaire *coup d'état* of 1799 (p. 88). But the important principle behind these details is that Fichte's constitutional proposals are made in the context of an imagined society of self-directed individuals each concerned with preserving his own sphere of action and interested in that of others only as a means of maintaining his own.[36] Fichte's state at the level of the understanding would be kept together by a multiplicity of regulations rather than by a common life and trust.[37]

VI

This brings us to what Hegel calls "absolute ethical life," and "absolute ethical totality," which, he says, "is nothing other than a *people*" (*Volk*), and the individual "proves his unity with the people unmistakeably through the danger of death alone" (p. 93). Peoples, he emphasizes, are not mere names, *entia rationis*, logical or intellectual constructions, but real individuals living alongside and in relative independence of one another. Fichte had argued that there could not be one free individual alone, but that there must essentially be a plurality of them.[38] Hegel transfers this idea from individual men to peoples, arguing that that very conception of a people necessitates the existence of a plurality of them. They are sometimes at peace with one another, sometimes at war, but "perpetual peace" (the title of Kant's famous pamphlet of 1795) would lead the institutions within each of these peoples to become static and lifeless and would bring on their ultimate decay.

Let us first consider the nature of these "absolute ethical totalities." Individual men belong to one of them insofar as they are required to risk their lives in military service. Some would regard this as an enslavement, but men could not be coerced into this unless there were a general sentiment to accept it. Locke's view that men tacitly show their choice of civil society merely by continuing to live in it would not, therefore, satisfy Hegel, who considers that the union is a much closer one. It is his view that they are related to the "ethical totality" much as organs are related to the body they belong to. The organs taken together are the body, and although the destruction of one or two of them may not destroy the body as a whole, they are nothing without it. Hegel says that particular men are "organs" of the "absolute ethical life" (p. 99), and that "the absolutely ethical has its own proper organic body in individuals" (p. 115). Perhaps his most striking statement of this point of view is that "the ethical life of the individual is one pulse beat of the whole system and is itself the whole system" (p. 112).

This is far removed from Hobbes's proudly self-seeking individuals and Fichte's prickly sticklers for their spheres of freedom. The argument about risking one's life is very important. Hobbes thought that civil society exists to provide security for each individual, but was embarrassed to explain why he should be called upon to serve in the army. He could pay someone else to serve in his place, he says, but this does not remove the irrationality of unnecessarily risking one's life to make one's life secure. To sacrifice one's life in order to make it secure would surely be nothing short of idiotic. It would seem reasonable, in the lights of the understanding, to leave self-sacrifice and death in battle to people who, unlike Falstaff, believe in honor. In an unpublished paper of 1795-6, now entitled *The Positivity of the Christian Religion*, Hegel had written that in Ancient Greece the citizens lived and lost their lives for their city because they could not conceive themselves as wanting to survive apart from it.[39] As we say today, they identified themselves with it or felt that they could not maintain their identities apart from it. Hegel's view is that morality and law belong in a community in which there are enough men who think and act like this to maintain it in being. Children are brought into this common life in the process of being educated. The child, says Hegel "is suckled at the breast of the universal ethical life; it lives first in an absolute vision of that life as alien to it, but comprehends it more and more and so passes over into the universal spirit" (p. 115). The structure of this universal ethical life is the permeation of the parts by the whole in which the parts exist to foster and develop.

In supporting this view Hegel says that it is manifested theoretically in Montesquieu's "immortal work," *L'Esprit des Lois*, in which the particular institutions of society are held to be explicable only in the light of the whole. According to Hegel, Montesquieu has shown that legality and legal systems cannot be derived from the application of some set of universal *a priori* principles, but must be exhibited in the light of "the living individuality of a nation" (a people, *Volk*) (p. 129). This throws light on two of Hegel's philosophical views at this time. In the first place it underlines his predilection for "pure" as distinct from "scientific" empiricism (p. 18 above, referring to p. 62, p. 67). His view is that someone who tries to set down *everything* about a society without selection may succeed in enabling his readers to become aware of the spirit of the whole. In the second place he thought that at the human level rational understanding consists in relating particular actions and institutions to the "ethical totality" in which they have their place rather than to universal laws. It is in the human sphere that Kant's Reason comes into its own, and the "totality" involved, being an historical people, makes it practical.

We must now turn to the more technically metaphysical elements in Hegel's theory of society, and ask how the individuals who belong to a people are related to the whole of which they are the body. We must first note that at this point we pass from the categories of relation to the categories of Reason, of the Concept (*Begriff*—p. 70), of the infinite (see Translator's Note on "Infinity"), for Hegel already had in mind, as his *Jena Logic* shows (see Note 15), a very general scheme which in 1812-3 became the *Science of Logic*. We have already seen that the relationships are organic, i.e., analogous to those between organs of a body, and between the organs and the life of the body. We have also seen that the organs are not organs apart from the body they belong to. They each contribute something different to it, yet cannot go their own way without upsetting the life of the whole. Hegel, it will be remembered, goes so far as to say not only that the individuals are pulses of the whole but that each individual *is* the whole. Surely, it will be objected, something cannot be both a part and the whole, an organ and the whole organism too. Hegel, however, is endeavoring to show that social relationships can only be understood in terms that are very different from the relations between physical particles or merely biological systems, and that, in particular, the social whole is "in" the individuals who belong to it.[40] This "in" is not spatial, because if it were, something that was "in" could not be "out" as well, which the social whole certainly is. In being educated, the individuals receive their knowledge and their aims and ideals from it, and they say what they say and do what they do because their country is what it is. Each from his point of view, to use the terminology of Leibniz, "reflects" the whole, or is a "perspective" of it. We find it extraordinary to say that the pulse *is* the whole, because we think of the pulse as a physical process of a physical thing, and physical things are themselves and nothing else. But an adult individual man is not merely his body; his education and his social functions and aims are aspects of the whole as well as aspects of him. In the language later used by Bradley and Bosanquet, each social individual transcends himself. Hegel illustrated his organic view very aptly in the *System der Sittlichkeit* when he there wrote: "This ethical life is a living, independent mind (*Geist*); it appears as a Briareus[41] with myriads of eyes, arms and other limbs, each one of which is an absolute individual and absolute universal; by reference to the individual, every part of this universality, everything that belongs to it, appears as an object, an end."[42]

This way of looking at society and the individual, Hegel believed, must influence the way in which we view the relation of law and the state to what is ordinarily called morality. Morality is often if not always regarded as a personal or interpersonal affair, concerned with the motives and intentions, the actions and virtues and vices of individual men and women. Hegel, however, quoting Aristotle's "The state comes by nature before the individual," holds that the virtues of individual men depend upon the ethical totality and ethical life which surrounds them. The virtues of individual men, he says, are "potentialities and have a negative meaning" (p. 113). Hegel's argument appears to be that these virtues would not exist apart from the ethical totality, and only become actual in individuals as they live the lives that the structure of their totality demands. In Bradley's language, the duties of the individual are settled by his station. It might be argued, indeed, that it is not only virtues that are determined by the whole, but also the types of action, since the very things that people can do depend upon the work and play that are there to be done. Hegel therefore reverses Fichte's account of morality and law. According to Fichte, morality is a matter of personal good will and law a matter of amorally coercing everyone into refraining from encroaching on the freedom of others.[43] According to Hegel, an individual can be virtuous because law and the state provide the paths and the directions.

In the course of this account of the virtues, Hegel makes a comment which seems to represent a stage in the development of his famous theory of "world-historical individuals" who recognize and facilitate a major shift in world history as did Alexander the Great, Julius Caesar, Luther, and Napoleon. He says (p. 114) that the virtues of such men as Epaminondas, Hannibal, and Caesar are, unlike those of ordinary men, more than merely negative potentialities and are "the stronger emergence of one aspect of the Idea of the whole." If the whole he has in mind is the "ethical totality," these pre-eminent virtues are of local rather than of world-historical significance. Certainly Hannibal's courage and resolution served

Carthage, but they went for nothing in the face of Roman power. Caesar, however, became a world-historical individual because he recognized that the Roman Republic *was* by his time a mere *ens rationis* or *Gedankending* and no longer an "ethical totality." In the next section we shall have to consider Hegel's view of history.

Before we come to this topic, however, we should briefly consider Hegel's account of classes and of the virtues associated with them. In effect he adapts, with modifications made necessary by the developing industrial revolution, the scheme of classes and virtues applied by Plato in the *Republic* to Ancient Greece. Plato divided his ideal society into three classes, the Guardians whose characteristic virtue is wisdom, the auxiliaries or fighting men whose characteristic virtue is courage, and the class of traders and workers whose characteristic virtue is temperance. Hegel's divisions and virtues are reached on a different principle, since he asks which class is free and which is not, and takes risking one's life as the criterion. The aristocratic or noble class, he says, has work to do, but not the work that consists in transforming raw materials for purposes of consumption. It is the twofold task of risking their lives in defense of the whole and developing the political life of the whole. In risking their lives they transcend nature and are free, and they inhabit the infinite and rational sphere of ethical life. The second class do not risk their lives but seek to accummulate wealth and to enjoy comfort. They are therefore not free and inhabit the world of the understanding with the state as a means to their personal satisfaction and with the bad infinity of unlimited gain as their inspiration. Obviously Hegel considered that Fichte did their legal theorizing for them. There is also a third class consisting of those who work on the land and do not in consequence have the knowledge of economic repercussions and relationships that the second class have. They are, however, ready to place their bodies at the service of the first class and fight uncomplainingly in their armies (p. 100). In the *System der Sittlichkeit* Hegel says that the virtue of the first class is courage, that of the second honesty and that of the third loyalty (*das Zutrauen*).[44]

Hegel has in this scheme recognized the great importance of the business class in modern society and recognized too that it must have high intelligence and cannot therefore be classed with manual workers as in Plato's *Republic*. The aristocracy, as he saw them, were not likely to take much interest in mathematics and metaphysics, but service in the army put everything they had at risk. If the peasants were disloyal or the outlook of the traders became universal the whole society would collapse. Under the Roman Empire the first class had capitulated and everyone, as Gibbon put it, had "sunk into the languid indifference of private life," and this could happen in modern society too if the second class developed at the expense of the others. The existence of the second class, Hegel jokingly says, is a sacrificial offering by the ethical life to the infernal powers to keep them in a good humor with the society as a whole and allow it to prosper (p. 103). "Dead" and "inorganic" as it is, it has its essential part to play.

VII

We have so far considered the relation of the individual man to the ethical totality which is a people, and have seen that according to Hegel there is necessarily a plurality of peoples sometimes at peace and sometimes at war with one another, and suffering in war the disturbances that prevent them from becoming stagnant and lifeless. It is clear from this that he was not in sympathy with the view of Kant and Fichte that human history is moving towards the happy establishment of agreements among the peoples which would provide the world with a cosmopolitan order. He writes, indeed, of "the shapelessness of cosmopolitanism," of "the void of the Rights of Man" and of "the like void of a league of nations or a world republic" (p. 132). It is interesting, in view of his association with Schelling, that in rejecting a league of nations Hegel was going against what Schelling had looked forward to in his *System of Transcendental Idealism*, in which he had written of a "State of States" and a "universal Areopagus of the peoples."[45] In this same work, Schelling, like Fichte, had said that "jurisprudence is not a part of ethics but a purely theoretical science which is in relation to freedom what mechanics is in relation to movement . . . thus the legal order is not a moral order but a mere natural order over which freedom is capable of as little as over sensible nature."[46] In spite of this fundamental difference Hegel makes use in the *Natural Law* essay of a good deal of Schelling's philosophical terminology and even writes as though he accepted Schelling's basic philosophical position on the absolute Substance and its attributes.

The *System of Transcendental Idealism* deals with two expressions of the absolute Substance. The first is theoretical and is concerned with unconscious physical nature, and the second is practical and deals with human history, which is the unpredictable realm of progress and of freedom. In the lectures (*The Methods of Academic Study*) he gave in 1802 when he was working closely with Hegel, he repeats this view and goes on to say that history is nature at a higher power (*Potenz*) and is "this great mirror of the world-spirit, this eternal poem of the divine understanding."[47]

In the *Natural Law* essay Hegel expounds as his own Schelling's metaphysics of the two expressions of Substance.[48] The first of these attributes, he says, is physical nature, in which plurality is more important than unity, and the second is ethical nature, in which unity prevails over multiplicity. As we have seen, his account of the individuals of ethical nature is very different from that of Schelling, but like him he writes of the "world-spirit" (p. 127) which becomes conscious of itself in the various peoples of history. He writes of "the tragedy which the Absolute eternally enacts with itself, by eternally giving birth to itself into objectivity, submitting in this objective form to suffering and death, and rising from its ashes into glory" (p. 104). He compares the various "shapes" which the world-spirit adopts to the totality of life which is present "in the nature of the polyp as in that of the nightingale and the lion" (p. 127). History as a whole is a tragedy because in history, as in tragedy, an inorganic element of necessity—like economic necessity within the ethical totality—is encountered as a fate with which the individual has to become reconciled. As Hegel sees it, this inorganic element is united with the divine substance in its ultimate unity (p. 104). This is what Hyppolite calls Hegel's "pantragism."[49] Can history be seen as a comedy too? Only, according to Hegel, if the element of fate is ignored. In Dante's *Divine Comedy* the consistent Thomistic balance gives God a victory against which there is no serious or justified opposition (p. 105). In secular comedy the characters do not wrestle with fate but with one another, and society is a field for human maneuver while "the Absolute is an illusion" (p. 108). As Hyppolite says, this type of comedy belongs to an individualistic society.

What Hegel subsequently called "world-history" is here in all but name.[50] Substance or the Absolute has two attributes, physical nature and ethical nature. The latter is the realm of freedom and of history. The "world-spirit" differentiates itself into "ethical totalities" or "peoples" which, through the courage of a few and the loyalty of many become living and flourishing individuals. Physical nature, necessity, and death, however, are always in them, are, indeed, required as oppositions to provoke activity. If the impulses towards the life of the whole slacken, or if mere elements or aspects become isolated (p. 123), or if institutions are allowed to ossify and outlive their time (p. 130-1), the people falls into decline or decay. But new ones will arise and the philosopher reconciles himself to the tragedy of it all with the reflection that if men did not risk their lives and meet with death there would be no freedom and no history.

Edinburgh   H. B. ACTON
1974

Notes

1. A photographic reproduction of this journal with a valuable Appendix by Hartmut Büchner was published in 1967 (Olms, Hildenheim). It is also reproduced in Hegel's *Gesammelte Werke*, vol. 4, ed. H. Büchner and O. Pöggeler, *Jenaer Kritische Schriften* (Hamburg, 1968).

2. Hegel uses this expression in the *Phenomenology of Mind* (1807) A, 3, Force and Understanding: Appearance and the Supersensible World.

3. *The Secret of Hegel*, 2 vols. (London, 1865), 1:24.

4. H. Nohl, *Hegels Theologische Jugendschriften* (Tübingen, 1907), p. 90.

5. G. W. F. Hegel, *Early Theological Writings*, trans. T. M. Knox, with an Introduction by Richard Kroner (Chicago, 1948; corrected edition with same pagination Philadelphia: U. of Pa. Press, 1971), pp. 81-2 (Nohl, pp. 102-3).

6. *Early Theological Writings*, pp. 214-6, p. 288 (Nohl, pp. 286-7, p. 331).

7. In *Perpetual Peace* Kant writes: ". . . it does not require that we know how to obtain the moral improvement of men but only that we should know the mechanism

of nature in order to use it on men, organizing the conflict of the hostile intentions present in a people in such a way that they must compel themselves to submit to coercive laws." Schelling writes: "Natural law . . . necessarily destroys itself; that is, it removes law altogether. For the ultimate to which it entrusts the upholding of law is physical superiority." *Neue Deduktion des Naturrechts* §162. *Sämmtliche Werke*, ed. K. F. A. S. Schelling (Stuttgart, 1856). Fichte writes: "If through a coercive law ruling with mechanical necessity every injury to the rights of the other becomes an injury to my own, I will take the same pains for the security of the other that I take for my own . . ." *Grundlage des Naturrechts* §14.

8. Hegel to Schelling, end of January, 1795. *Briefe von und an Hegel* (ed. J. Hoffmeister, 1952) 1:18

9. *Differenzschrift*. Section headed "The Need for Philosophy." *Gesammelte Werke*, 4:12.

10. Ibid., p. 59. On p. 15 Hegel writes of "the struggle of the understanding with reason."

11. *Naturrecht oder Rechts-Philosophie als die praktische Philosophie enthaltend Rechts-, Sitten-, und Gesellschaftslehre*, 2 vols. (Berlin, 1866).

12. *Neue Deduktion des Naturrechts*, pp. 161–2.

13. Karl Rosenkranz, *Hegels Leben* (Berlin, 1844), pp. 189ff. Heinz Kimmerle, Dokumente zu Hegels Dozententätigkeit 1801–7, in *Hegel Studien* 4 (Bonn, 1967). Heinz Kimmerle, *Das Problem der Abgeschlossenheit des Denkens: Hegels "System der Philosophie" in den Jahren 1800–1804, Hegel Studien*, 8 (Bonn, 1970).

14. Rosenkranz, pp. 190–191.

15. Hegel, *Gesammelte Werke*, vol. 7, *Jenaer Systementwürfe II* (Hamburg, 1971).

16. Ibid., p. 31.

17. Ibid., p. 38.

18. Allen W. Wood, *Kant's Moral Religion* (Ithaca and London, 1970), pp. 3-4.

19. Rosenkranz, pp. 86–88 for Hegel's commentary on Kant's *Metaphysic of Morals*, and pp. 88–90 for his discussion of the "world-crisis" and the constitution of Germany. This second passage also appears in *Schriften zur Politik und Rechtsphilosophie*, ed. Lasson (Leipzig, 1913), pp. 138–141. It is discussed by H. S. Harris in *Hegel's Development: Towards the Sunlight, 1770–1801* (Oxford, 1972), pp. 440–5. For details of Hegel's views on the constitution of Germany see *Hegel's Political Writings*, trans. T. M. Knox, ed. Z. A. Pelczynski (Oxford, 1964).

20. W. H. Walsh, *Hegelian Ethics* (London, 1969), pp. 22–7.

21. Marcus Singer, *Generalisation in Ethics: An Essay in the Logic of Ethics with the Rudiments of a System of Moral Philosophy* (London, 1963), pp. 251–253. A valuable discussion.

22. *Phenomenology* (trans. Baillie) pp. 619-20. For the alleged "shiftiness" of Kantian *Moralität*, see *Phenomenology* (trans. Baillie), pp. 629ff., section headed "Dissemblance" ("Verstellung"). Hegel's relationship to Kant in these criticisms is analyzed and discussed by Sir Malcolm Knox in "Hegel's Attitude to Kant's Ethics," *Kant Studien* 49 (1957-8). See also W. H. Walsh's *Hegelian Ethics* (London, 1969), p. 33. F. H. Bradley discusses the *Natural Law* essay's treatment of the "paradox of morality" in *Ethical Studies*, 2nd ed., pp. 151ff.

23. The practical points at issue are discussed by W. H. Walsh in "Open and Closed Morality" in *The Morality of Politics* (ed. B. Parekh and R. N. Berki, London, 1972), especially pp. 20-1 and p. 27. The paragraphs in the *Natural Law* essay immediately following p. 80 are difficult to interpret. The use of "perception" (*Anschauung*) is

borrowed from Schelling who employs the word in his *System of Transcendental Idealism* (1800). The passage Hegel seems to have in mind is concerned with our perception of human actions which, Schelling had said, must be perceived in the natural working of human bodies regarded as subject to human impulses "(through pain [*Schmerz*] in its most general meaning), and all action, in order to be objective, must, however many intermediaries there may be, be in agreement with a physical compulsion which is itself necessary as a condition of freedom as it appears [in the natural world]." *Sämmtliche Werke*, 1, section 3:571. Schelling is trying to give an acceptable interpretation of Kant's view of freedom as the noumenal world acting on the phenomenal world, and Hegel (pp. 81ff.) is arguing that such a "two world" view of morality becomes immorality if there is this opposition between what is done in the natural world and a noumenal cause of it.

24. The distinction between abstract and concrete universals is important here. Hegel discusses the distinction, without using the terminology, on pp. 108-15 below. An abstract universal is an identical character qualifying all the members of a class of particulars. A concrete universal is the identical spirit shared and exhibited by all the individuals of a system. Abstract universals may be unimportant characteristics of the particulars they belong to; for example, it does not matter to the contents of a book whether its cover is yellow or blue in color. Concrete universals belong essentially to their individual embodiments; for example, visible surfaces must have some color, and individual Frenchmen must carry with them the history and structure of France (i.e., French cooking in French Equatorial Africa). According to Hegel, in Kant's conception of "all men" or of "world citizens," individual men are regarded as members of a class sharing common characteristics, but apart from this the individuals are separate from one another; the citizens of a state, on the other hand, share a common life, to which each makes his own specific contribution. All men, or humanity at large, is an amorphous and artificial multiplicity. France, or the United States of America, is a natural whole possessing a structure of classes and institutions. Hegel developed the contrast between abstract and concrete universals in his *Science of Logic* (1812-13), Book 1, section 1, chapter 1, and his *Encyclopedia* §§160-165. In his *Philosophy of Right* (1821) he held that the state is a concrete universal. For his account of concrete universals in that work see §24 and §49 with Knox's notes, p. 319 and pp. 322-4. Klaus Hartmann in *Die Marxsche Theorie* (Bonn, 1970), pp. 97-101 and *passim* emphasizes the concrete universality of the state in Hegel's philosophy. See also: H. B. Acton "The Theory of Concrete Universals," *Mind* 45 & 46, nos. 180 & 181 (1936 and 1937).

25. Fichte, *Werke*, I, 3 (Stuttgart-Bad Canstatt, 1966)—*Grundlage des Naturrechts* 4:359. On p. 360 he writes: "Both sciences are independently basic (*Ursprünglich*) and distinguished by the reason without any interference on our part and are completely opposed to one another."

26. Fichte, *Werke* 1, section 3:425.

27. Ibid., p. 426.

28. Ibid., pp. 425-6.

29. Ibid., p. 427.

30. Ibid., p. 446.

31. Hegel, *Gesammelte Werke*, 4:58.

32. Fichte, *Werke*, 1, section 3:425-6.

33. 1133[a]

34. *System der Sittlichkeit*, Reprinted, 1967, from Lasson's edition of Hegel's

Schriften zur Politik und Rechtsphilosophie (2nd ed. Hamburg, 1923), pp. 41ff. I have summarized the main aspects of a very complex argument.

35. This is brilliantly discussed by Hegel in the *Philosophy of Right*, §140.

36. Hegel, *Gesammelte Werke*, 4:56.

37. Schelling, in his *Lectures on the Methods of Academic Study* (delivered at Jena in 1802 and published in book form in 1803, 1811 and 1830) writes, with reference to Fichte's *Naturrecht:* "The selection of the merely finite side extends the organism of the constitution into an endless mechanism in which nothing unconditioned is found. In general, all previous attempts can be criticized for the character of dependence they give to the state, that is, the idea that the state is established *in order that* this or that end should be secured. Whether this end is regarded as the general happiness, as satisfaction of the social impulses of human nature, or as something purely formal, such as the association of free beings under the conditions of the maximum possible freedom, is in this context a matter of complete indifference; for in all these cases the state is conceived as merely a means, as conditioned and dependent" (*Sämmtliche Werke*, 1, section 5:316). Schelling has accepted Hegel's view of Fichte's *Naturrecht*.

38. *Grundlage des Naturrechts*, §3. See especially corollary I: "Man (and finite beings generally) becomes a man only among men . . . *if in general there are to be men, there must be a plurality of them* . . . . The concept of man is thus not the concept of a particular, because this is unthinkable, but of a species." *Werke*, 1, section 3:347.

39. *Early Theological Writings* (trans. Knox), pp. 154–5, Nohl, pp. 221–2. This is in Part II of *The Positivity of the Christian Religion*. Part III was written later.

40. This aspect of the matter is brilliantly discussed by F. H. Bradley in *Ethical Studies* (1876), where it is argued that Mill and Bain have a view of the mind based on the concepts of mechanics. In *Ethical Studies* Bradley refers on several occasions to Hegel's *Natural Law* essay, which impressed him greatly. But he was not the first in England to be so impressed. The review of J. S. Mill's *On Liberty* (1859) in the *National Review* of that year advocated an organic view of society against the views of Mill, and stated: "Society has, and ought to have, a common life, which sends its pulse through every individual soul."—quoted in J. C. Rees, *Mill and his Early Critics*, (Leicester: University College, 1956). My guess is that the review was written by John Oxenford, a Hegelian who also contributed to the German Hegelian periodical *Der Gedanke*, founded in 1860.

41. A fifty-headed and hundred-handed monster.

42. p. 56. The great multiplicity of limbs and of eyes looking at and being looked at by other eyes gives a picture of Hegel's view of society.

43. In later writings such as *Der Geschlossene Handelsstaat* (1800), Fichte confirmed Hegel's forebodings about his progress towards the support of despotism. On the development of Fichte's political philosophy away from his earlier liberalism see G. A. Kelly's *Idealism, Politics and History: Sources of Hegelian Thought* (Cambridge, 1969).

44. *System der Sittlichkeit*, pp. 63–8.

45. Schelling, *Werke*, 1, section 3:586–7.

46. Ibid., p. 583.

47. Schelling, *Werke*, 1, section 5:309. See footnote 37.

48. See Manfred Riedel, "Hegels Kritik des Naturrechts" in *Hegel-Studien* 4 (Bonn, 1967).

49. Jean Hyppolite, *Introduction à la Philosophie de l'Histoire de Hegel* (Paris, 1948), p. 78.

50. He uses the term in 1805–6 in the *Jenenser Realphilosophie*, II (Leipzig, 1931), p. 273. I do not know when the term "world-history" was first used, but Schiller used it in his Inaugural Lecture to the Chair of History at Jena in 1789. Schiller had also used the expression in his poem *Resignation* (1785) in the line: "Die Weltgeschichte is das Weltgericht"—"World-history is the world's court of judgment." Kant uses the expression "world-history" in his *Idea for a Universal History* (1784). Courses on "universal history" were given in universities at this time. It is significant that Schiller wrote both historical works on such topics as the revolt in the Netherlands and historical tragedies such as his *Mary Stuart*.

Translator's Note

This translation is based on Hegel's original periodical publication, now reprinted in the magnificient new edition of his Works. See vol. 4, ed. by H. Büchner and O. Pöggeler (Hamburg, 1968). The page references in the foot of the translation are to the pages of this edition. One or two references in my notes to this edition are described as "Pöggeler". However I have adopted some minor emendations to the text from the first edition of the collected Works and from the edition by G. Lasson (Leipzig, 1923). All the material enclosed in square brackets, whether in the text or the footnotes, is the translator's.

A German scholar (*Hegel-Studien* 4 [Bonn, 1967], p. 177) refers to the "obscurities" in this essay, but unfortunately he does not provide the new light which might remove them, and this translation does not profess to remove them either. For substantial help I am much indebted to Professor Acton for his introduction, to Dr. Z. A. Pelczynski and Dr. R. Hausherr for reading and improving and correcting the translation.

The obscurities in the essay arise partly from the abstraction on which Hegel always prided himself, and partly from the terminology. In 1802 he had not worked out his own but used terms drawn from Schelling and others; and he makes things more difficult by sometimes using a word in its ordinary German sense, and sometimes in his own technical sense. This is the case, for example with *Sittlichkeit* which means "morality," but later in the essay the distinction—clear in the later *Philosophy of Right*—from *Moralität* occurs, and therefore I use "ethical life" to translate the word, where "morality" would be more natural in English. And yet there are times when "morality," instead of "ethics" etc., seems imperative.

With hesitation I offer some comments on terminology:

Anschauung—"intuition" in translations of Kant has become familiar. But although I have accepted this rendering at times, I have used, with misgivings, "perception," or "view." A lot may depend on the context. But when Hegel asserts that in *Anschauung* "particular and universal are identified," he seems almost to mean by the word what he later calls "reason," and we are reminded of Schelling's *System of Transcendental Idealism* (Tübingen, 1800), p. 50: "A knowing which is at the same time a production of its object is an *intuition* . . . not sensuous but intellectual intuition, the organ of all transcendental thinking."

Absolute form is apparently "the concrete form of the Absolute"; thinking must embody itself in something concrete or it has no substantiality.

Verhältnis: "relation." So translated, or where the terms of the relation are not specified, "relationships" (but reference should be made to Hegel's *Jenenser Logik* in *Ges. Werke* [edn. cit. above], vol. 7 [Hamburg, 1971].)

Indifferenz—*indifference.* This Schellingian term seems to mean "identity."

Negative absolute or identity. The negative absolute, unlike the true Absolute which is a unity of form and content, is a pure abstraction, the empty concept of unity. It is "infinite" in the sense that it is an endless succession of negatives. For example, morality is concrete and specific, but the immoral is vague and indefinite. There is one way to hit the mark, but many ways of missing it. A negative absolute, renouncing any concrete content, rejects from it, as immoral, *ad infinitum* anything that does not correspond with it.

Absolute concept. This is obscure. At one point it is identified with the "negative absolute." In Hegel's *Aesthetics* it is clearly a synonym for "God." It is not impossible that here it is identified with God as purely transcendent and therefore as the negative of the created world, though the indwelling essence, or concept, of that world.

Infinity. Here problems multiply. At one point, for example, limitations have the form of infinity. This can only mean, so far as I can see, that limitations have no end. But, in that case "infinity" is what Hegel calls later (and did in his Jena manuscripts at much the same date as this essay) the "bad" infinite, i.e. what goes on and on in a straight line instead of returning into itself like a circle. Yet elsewhere, "infinite" seems to be the genuine infinite which is not just the negation of this and this and this *ad infinitum*, but which returns into itself out of these negations as the truly positive. This is one of the cases where Hegel seems to use a word now in one sense and now in another.

It was at the suggestion of the late Mr. Fred Wieck, then Director of the University of Pennsylvania Press, that this translation was made, and I now record my gratitude to him for his encouragement and to his staff for help with revisions of my work. He was himself no mean Hegelian scholar, and it is very sad that he is no longer here to see the book published. I am also indebted to Dr. John R. Silber, President of Boston University and the Editor of the Series in which this book appears. His editorship has been no sinecure and I am grateful to him for his watchful care and for the numerous suggestions which have led to improvements in the translation.

This translation was completed in 1972 and revised in 1974 shortly before Professor Acton's death. The final revision, now completed, has not had the benefit of his advice. I am deeply indebted to him for writing the Introduction at my request. His loss is a severe blow to Hegelian studies and, indeed, to philosophy generally.

My share in this book I now dedicate to his memory.

Crieff   T. M. Knox
March, 1975

The Scientific Ways of Treating Natural Law, Its Place in Moral Philosophy, and Its Relation to the Positive Sciences of Law ❧

The science of natural law, like other sciences such as mechanics and physics, has long been recognized as an essentially philosophical science and, since philosophy must have parts, as an essential part of philosophy. But with the other sciences it has shared a common fate; the philosophical element in philosophy is assigned exclusively to metaphysics, while the sciences have been allowed little share in it. On the contrary, in their special principle they have been kept aloof in complete independence of the Idea. In the end, the sciences cited as examples have been compelled more or less to confess their removal from philosophy. As a result they acknowledge that what is commonly called "experience" is their scientific principle and therefore they renounce their claim to be genuine sciences. They are content to consist of a collection of empirical observations and to make use of the categories of the understanding only as suppliants, without wishing to assert anything objective.

If, originally against its will, what had called itself a philosophical science was shut out of philosophy and, generally, the category of science, and if in the end it has accepted this position, the reason for this exclusion is not that, although these so-called sciences issued from philosophy itself, they failed to maintain a conscious connection with it. For every part of philosophy is capable in its individuality of being an independent science and acquiring a complete inner necessity of its own, since it is the Absolute which makes philosophy a genuine science. In this form the Absolute alone is the special principle which lies above the sphere of science's knowledge and freedom, and, by relation to this principle, the science is possessed by an external necessity. But the Idea itself remains free of this determinacy and it can be reflected in this determinate science just as purely as absolute life is expressed in every living thing, though the scientific element in such a science, or its inner rationality, does not come to light in the pure form of the Idea, which is the essence of every science and which in philosophy, as the absolute science, is present as this pure Idea. Of this independent and yet free scientific development of a science, geometry supplies a brilliant example that is the envy of the other sciences. All the same, it does not follow that sciences like those mentioned above must be denied all reality because they are, strictly speaking, empirical. For just as each part or aspect of philosophy is capable of being an independent science, so each such science is thus immediately an independent and perfect picture and, in the form of a picture, can be accepted and expounded by an intuition which purely and happily keeps itself free from contamination by fixed concepts.

But the perfection of the science requires not only that perception and picture be united with the logical element and taken up into the purely ideal, but also that the separate, though genuine, science be stripped of its separateness; its principle must be recognized in its higher context and necessity, and thus and only thus be completely freed. In this way alone is it possible to know the limits of the science; and without this principle the science must remain ignorant of its limits, because otherwise it would have to be superior to itself and recognize the nature of its principle according to its determinate character in the absolute form. For from this knowledge the science would derive directly the knowledge and certainty of the extent of the equality of its various specifications. But, as it is, its attitude to its own limits can only be empirical, and it must now make vain attempts to go beyond them, now think them narrower than they are, and thus experience wholly unexpected extensions of scope, as happens even in geometry (which, e.g., can prove the incommensurability of the diameter [diagonal] and the side of the square, but not that of the diameter and the circumference of a circle),° and even more in arithmetic; and, most of all, geometry and arithmetic in combination provide the greatest example of science fumbling in the dark along its borders.

°In the Introduction to his *Naturrecht* [Introduction §1, fn. 2], Fichte makes much of the simplicity of insight into the reason for this latter incommensurability: "Curved is in fact just not straight." The superficiality of this reason is obvious at once, and it is also refuted immediately by the former incommensurability (diagonal and side of the square) because both of these are straight lines, and also by the square of the parabola. As for the help sought in the same context from "healthy common sense" against the mathematical infinite, that "a many-angled figure with an infinite number of sides cannot be measured simply because it is a many-angled figure with an infinite number of sides," (a) the very same resource would have to be available against the infinite progression in which the absolute Idea is supposed to be realized, and (b) by this means there is no settling whether the chief thing at issue, positive infinity (which is identity, not an infinite multitude), is to be granted. And this is as good as saying that nothing is settled either concerning commensurability or incommensurability.

The Critical philosophy has had the important *negative* effect on theoretical sciences of proving that the scientific element in them is not objective, but belongs to a middle realm between nothing and reality, to a mixture of being and not-being, and thus making them admit that they belong only to the sphere of empirical thinking. The *positive* effect of the Critical philosophy has turned out all the poorer in proportion, and it has not been able to recover these sciences for philosophy. On the other hand, the Critical philosophy has placed the Absolute wholly within practical philosophy, and there the Critical philosophy is positive or dogmatic knowledge. We must regard the Critical philosophy (which also calls itself transcendental idealism) in general, and particularly in natural law, as the culminating point of that opposition which (like circles on the surface of water spreading outward concentrically from the point where the surface was disturbed and finally, in small movements, losing their relation to a center and going on *ad infinitum*) from feeble beginnings in earlier scientific endeavours, outgrew the confinement of barbarism and became ever greater until it reached understanding of itself in the Critical philosophy by means of the absolute concept of infinity and, as infinity, now also cancels itself.*

The earlier ways of treating natural law, and also what would have to be regarded as its various principles, must therefore be denied all significance for the essence of science, because their element is opposition and negativity, yet not absolute negativity (i.e., infinity) which alone is the element for science; on the contrary, they no more possess the purely positive than they do the purely negative, but are mixtures of both. Only one curious about the history of science could be interested enough to linger over them in order, first, to compare them with the absolute Idea and to discern in their distortion the necessity whereby, intertwined with a

---

*[Elsewhere Hegel identifies the "absolute concept" with both "infinity" and "reason." His continual complaint about Kant is that he sharply distinguishes opposites (e.g., finite and infinite) but never succeeds in synthesizing them. The meaning of this perplexing sentence may be that an earlier medieval opposition (e.g., between God and man) became intensified into other oppositions (e.g., between attraction and repulsion, freedom and necessity) until Kant made this opposition clear to itself in the categories of the Understanding, and it is now cancelled in the true synthesis of opposites which infinity is.]

determinate principle, the moments of absolute form are distortedly displayed and yet dominate these attempts even under the dominion of a narrow principle, and, second, to see the empirical condition of the world reflected in the ideal mirror of science.

As for the *second*, it is of course true that, since all things are interconnected, empirical existence and the condition of all sciences will express also the condition of the world. But the condition of natural law will do so in particular because natural law bears directly on the ethical, the mover of all things human; and, insofar as the science of ethics has an existence, it is under the necessity of being one with the empirical shape of the ethical, a shape equally necessary. And, as science, natural law must express that shape in the form of universality.

As for the *first*, the only true distinction that can be acknowledged as marking the principle of the science is whether the science lies within the Absolute, or outside absolute unity (i.e., in opposition). If the latter, it simply could not be science if its principle were not some incomplete and relative unity or the concept of a relation, even if the principle were only the empty abstraction of relation itself under the name of attractive force or the force of identity. In sciences whose principle is not a concept of relation, or only the empty force of identity, there remains nothing ideal except the first ideal relation, the way the child is different from the world, as with the form of picture-thinking in which the sciences place empirical qualities and can rehearse their variety—these sciences would be called pre-eminetly empirical sciences. But because practical sciences bear by their nature on some real universal or on a unity which is a unity of differences, the feelings too must comprise in practical empiricism not pure qualities but relations, be they negative like the urge to self-preservation, or positive like love and hate, sociability, and the like. And a more scientific empiricism differs from this pure empiricism, not in general by having as its object relations rather than qualities, but rather by fixing these relations in conceptual form and clinging to this negative absoluteness, though without severing this form of unity from its content. These we will call *empirical sciences*, while we term a purely *formal* science that form of science in which the opposition of form and content is absolute, and pure unity (or infinity, the negative absolute) is wholly separated from the content and posited independently.

Although there is thus established, between the two spurious ways of treating natural law scientifically, a specific difference whereby the principles of the one are relations and mixtures of empirical perception with the universal (while the principle of the other is absolute opposition and absolute universality), it is obvious nonetheless that the ingredients of both empirical perception and concept are the same, and that formalism, in passing over from its pure negation to a content, can likewise arrive at nothing else than relations or relative identities. Because the purely ideal or the opposition is absolutely posited, the absolute Idea and unity cannot be present. With the principle of absolute opposition, or of the absoluteness of the purely ideal, the absolute principle of empiricism is posited; and therefore, with reference to perception, the syntheses, insofar as they are not supposed to have just the purely negative meaning of annulling one side of the opposition but also a positive meaning of perception, portray only empirical perceptions.

These two ways of treating natural law scientifically must *first of all* be characterized in more detail, the first with reference to the manner in which the absolute Idea appears in it according to the moments of absolute form, the second with reference to the manner in which the infinite, or the negative absolute, vainly attempts to achieve a positive organization. The analysis of the latter attempt will lead directly to treating the nature and relation of the sciences of the ethical as philosophical sciences, and to their relation with what is called the positive science of law. The latter holds itself aloof from philosophy and, by voluntarily renouncing philosophy, imagines that it can avoid philosophy's criticism; yet it also claims to have absolute subsistence and true reality—a pretension not to be condoned.

As for that way of treating natural law which we have called *empirical*, the first point is that we cannot concern ourselves with the matter of the determinacies and relational concepts which it seizes upon and asserts under the name of principles. On the contrary, this separation and fixation of determinacies is just what must be negated. The nature of this separation implies that the scientific procedure applies only to the form of unity; and in an organic relation to the manifold qualities into which the unity is divided (if they are not simply to be enumerated), one certain determinate aspect must be emphasized in order to reach a unity over this multiplicity; and that determinate aspect must be regarded as the essence of the relation. But the totality of the organic is precisely what cannot be thereby attained, and the remainder of the relation, excluded from the determinate aspect that was selected, falls under the dominion of this aspect which is elevated to be the essence and purpose of the relation. Thus, for example, to explain the relation of marriage, procreation, the holding of goods in common, or something else is proposed [as the determinant] and, from such a determinate aspect, is made prescriptive as the essence of the relation; the whole organic relation is delimited and contaminated. Or, in the case of punishment, one specific aspect is singled out—the criminal's moral reform, or the damage done, or the effect of his punishment on others, or the criminal's own notion of the punishment before he committed the crime, or the necessity of making this notion a reality by carrying out the threat, etc. And then some such single aspect is made the purpose and essence of the whole. The natural consequence is that, since such a specific aspect has no necessary connection with the other specific aspects which can be found and distinguished, there arises an endless struggle to find the necessary bearing and predominance of one over the others; and since inner necessity, non-existent in singularity, is missing, each aspect can perfectly well vindicate its independence of the others.

Such qualities, taken up out of the multiplicity of the relation into which the organic is fragmented by empirical or inadequately reflective perception and put into the form of a conceptual unity, are what knowledge of this kind calls essence and purposes. And since their form of the Concept is expressed as the absolute being of the specific character constituting the content of the Concept, they are set up as principles, laws, duties, etc. Of this conversion of the absoluteness of pure form (which, however, is negative absoluteness or pure identity; the pure Concept; infinity) into the absoluteness of the content (and the determinacy taken into the form), more will be said in connection with the principle of the Critical philosophy. In the empirical knowledge which is here in question, this conversion comes about unconsciously, while the Critical philosophy enters upon it reflectively and as absolute reason and duty.

This formal unity, into which the determinacy is placed by thinking, also provides the appearance of that necessity which science strives for. For the unity of opposites in relation to science, regarded as a real unity, is science's necessity. But because the matter of this formal unity is not the whole of the opposites but only one of them (i.e., only one determinacy), the necessity too is only formal and analytic and is concerned only with the form of an identical or analytic proposition in which the determinacy can be presented. But by this absoluteness of the proposition an absoluteness of content too is smuggled in, and in this way laws and principles are constituted.

But this empirical science finds itself surrounded by a multiplicity of such principles, laws, ends, duties, and rights, none of which is absolute. It thus is bound also to conceive the picture of, and need for, the absolute unity of all these disconnected characteristics, and of an original simple necessity. We are considering how it will satisfy this demand rooted in reason, or how the absolute Idea of reason will be displayed in its moments when it is under the domination of what, for this empirical knowledge, is the insuperable opposition of the one and the many. For one thing, it is interesting in itself to discern in this scientific endeavour, and its murky medium, not only the reflection and the domination of the Absolute, but also its perversion. For another thing, the forms which the moments of the Absolute have received here turn into a species of prejudices and indubitable and universally valid thought whose nullity criticism must expose in order to justify science for ignoring them. This proof of their nullity is presented most convincingly by showing the unreal basis and ground from which they grow, and whose flavor and nature they absorb.

At first, empirical science envisages scientific totality as a totality of the multiplex or as completeness; while a strict formalism envisages it as consistency. The former can at will elevate its experiences to universality, and can push the consistency of its putative determinations up to the point where other empirical matter (which contradicts the first but has just as much right to be excogitated and expressed as a principle) no longer leaves room for the consistency of the preceding, and compels its abandonment. Formalism can extend its consistency so far as is generally made possible by the emptiness of its principle, or by a content which it has smuggled in; but thereby it is in turn entitled to exclude what lacks completeness from its apriorism and its science, and proudly revile it as "the empirical." For formalism asserts its formal principles as the *a priori* and absolute, and thus asserts that what it cannot master by these is non-absolute and accidental—unless it saves itself by finding in the empirical field generally (and in the movement from one characteristic to another) the formal transition of progression from the conditioned to the condition and, since the latter is in turn conditioned, so on *ad infinitum*. In this process, formalism not only abandons all its advantages over what it calls empiricism; rather, since in the context of the conditioned with the condition these opposites are posited as subsisting absolutely, formalism itself is completely submerged in empirical necessity and by means of the formal identity or negative absolute whereby it holds opposites together, endows empirical necessity with a resemblance of genuine absoluteness.

But this linking of consistency with the completeness of the picture—whether of the latter, more complete, formal and empty consistency, or of the former consistency which, with specific concepts as principles, proceeds from one of them to others and is consistent only in inconsistency—immediately alters the place of multiplicity in pure empiricism. For pure empiricism, everything has equal rights with everything else; one characteristic is as real as another, and none has precedence. We shall return to this point later when we compare pure empiricism with our present topic, scientific empiricism.

In this formal totality we must consider how absolute unity appears both as simple unity, which we may call the original unity, and as totality in the mirror of empirical knowing. Both unities, which are one in the Absolute and whose identity is the Absolute, must occur in such knowledge as separate and different from one another.

As for absolute unity, as that essence of necessity which for appearance is an external bond, the first point is that empiricism can have nothing to say about it; for in the unity which is the essential one, the multiplex is immediately annihilated and is null. Since multiplex being is the principle of empiricism, empiricism is precluded from pressing on to the absolute nullity of its qualities which for it are absolute and which besides, owing to the concept in accordance with which they are many, are infinitely many. This original unity can therefore mean, so far as possible, only a single, simple, and small mass of qualities, whereby it believes it can suffice for a knowledge of the rest. In that ideal, empiricism, in which what thus passes vaguely for capricious and accidental is blurred, and the smallest indispensable mass of the multiplex is posited; it is *chaos* in the physical as in the ethical world. Chaos in the latter is conceived now by the imagination more in the image of existence, as the *state of nature*, now by empirical psychology more in the form of potentiality and abstraction, as a list of the capacities found in man, as the *nature and destiny of man*. In this way, what on the one hand is asserted to be simply necessary in itself, absolute, is at the same time acknowledged on the other hand to be something not real, purely imaginary, an *ens rationis*—in the first case to be fiction, in the second a mere possibility; and this is the harshest contradiction.

For the ordinary understanding, which holds to the murky confusion of what is essential with the transitory, nothing is more understandable than its ability to find the essential thing in this way: namely that by separating out everything capricious and accidental from the confused picture of the *state of law*, it must after this abstraction be left directly with the absolutely necessary. If we think away everything that someone's obscure inkling may reckon amongst the particular and the transitory as belonging to particular manners, to history, to civilization, and even to the state, then what remains is man in the image of the bare state of nature, or the abstraction of man with his essential potentialities; and we have only to look in order to find what is necessary. What is seen to be connected with the state must therefore also be abstracted, because the chaotic picture of the necessary cannot contain absolute unity but only simple multiplicity, atoms with the fewest possible properties; and so, what can fall under the concept of a linking and ordering of these, the weakest unity of which the principle of multiplicity is capable, is therefore excluded as something that only comes later and is added on to that multiplicity.

Now in this separation [of unity from multiplicity] empiricism lacks in the first place all criteria for drawing the boundary between the accidental and the necessary; i.e., for determining what in the chaos of the state of nature or in the abstraction of man must remain and what must be discarded. In this matter the guiding determinant can only be, that as much must remain as is required for the exposition of what is found in the real world: the governing principle for this *a priori* is the *a posteriori*. If something in the idea of the state of law is to be justified, all that is required, for the purpose of demonstrating its own necessity and its connection with what is original and necessary, is to transfer into the chaos an appropriate quality or capacity and, in the manner of all the sciences based on the empirical, to make, for purposes of so-called explanation of reality, hypotheses in which this reality is posited in the same determinate character, though only in a formal-ideal shape as force, matter, capacity, etc. Any one of these is very readily made intelligible and explicable in terms of the other.

In one way this obscure inkling of original and absolute unity which is expressed in the chaos of the state of nature and in the abstraction of capacities and inclinations, does not achieve absolute negative unity but aims only at the extinction of a large multitude of particularities and oppositions. But there remains over and above in this chaos an indeterminable multitude of qualitative specifications which in themselves have only an empirical necessity, and not an inner necessity, for one another. They are only related as many, and, since the many are many for one another but without unity, they are destined to be self-opposed and to be in absolute conflict with one another. The separated energies of the ethical sphere must, in the state of nature or in the abstraction of man, be thought of as engaged in a war of mutual destruction. But, for this very reason, it is easy to show that since these qualities are flatly opposed to one another and so are purely ideal, they cannot subsist (as they are supposed to) in this ideality and separation, but simply cancel each other out and are reduced to nullity. But empiricism cannot attain to this absolute reflection or to an insight into the nullity of the characteristics in the absolutely simple; the many nullities remain for it a mass of realities. But to this multiplicity, the positive unity (expressing itself as absolute totality) must for empiricism be tacked on as something other and alien; and even this form of the linkage of the two sides of absolute identity implies that their totality will be displayed just as murkily and impurely as that of the original unity.

Empiricism does not find it difficult to offer grounds for one of these separated unities being for the other, or for the transition from one to the other, just as empiricism has in general no difficulty in offering grounds. After the fiction of the state of nature has served its purpose, that state is abandoned because of its ill consequences; this simply means that the desired outcome is presupposed, the outcome namely of an harmonization of what, as chaos, is in conflict with the good or whatever goal must be reached. Alternatively, a ground of transition is introduced directly into the idea of original qualities as potentialities, such as the gregarious instinct; or the conceptual form of "faculty" is abandoned, and one proceeds at once to the purely particular side of the appearance of the second unity (i.e., to something historical) such as the subjection of the weaker by the stronger, etc. But the unity itself can only proceed, as in empirical physics, according to the principle of an absolute quantitative multiplicity; in place of the many atomic qualities it can only exhibit a multiplicity of parts or relations—once again nothing but multiplex complexities of the presupposedly original simple and separated multiple units, superficial contacts between these qualities which in themselves are indestructible in their particularity and capable of only light and partial interconnections and intermixtures. Insofar as the unity is posited as a whole, it is given the empty name of a formless and external harmony called "society" and "state."

Even if the unity, whether in itself or regarded more empirically in relation to its emergence, is represented as absolute (deriving its immediate origin from God), and even if the center and inner essence of its existence may be represented as divine, this idea still remains something formal, merely hovering over the multiplicity, not penetrating it. Let God be recognized not only as the founder of the association but also as its upholder, and in relation to the latter let the majesty of the supreme power be recognized as his reflection and in itself divine. Even then the divine element in the association is something external for the associated many who must be placed in relation to that element only as under its dominion, since the principle of this empiricism excludes the absolute unity of the one and the many. At this point of the relation, empiricism coincides with its opposite principle for which abstract unity is the first thing, except that empiricism is not embarrassed by its inconsistencies arising from the mixture of things posited as specifically different, such as abstract unity and absolute multiplicity. For this very reason, it has the advantage of not closing the door to views which, apart from their purely material side, are appearances of a purer and more divine inner principle than can occur on the principle of opposition under which alone mastery and obedience are possible.

The state of nature, and that majesty and divinity of the whole state of law which is alien to individuals and therefore is single and particular (as well as the subject's situation of absolute subjection under this supreme power), are the forms in which the fragmented moments of organic ethical life (*Sittlichkeit*) are fixed as particular essences and thereby distorted, just as the Idea is: these moments are (i) the moment of absolute unity, and of absolute totality in so far as it incorporates the opposition of unity and multiplicity, and (ii) the moment of infinity, the nullifying of the realities of this opposition. The absolute Idea of ethical life, on the other hand, contains both majesty and the state of nature as simply identical, since the former is nothing but absolute ethical *nature;* and in the realization of majesty there can be no thought of any loss of absolute freedom, which is what would have to be understood by "natural freedom," or of any sacrifice of ethical nature. But the natural, which would have to be regarded in an ethical relation as something to be sacrificed, would itself not be ethical and so could least of all represent the ethical in its origin. Neither is infinity, or the negation of individuals or subjects, fixed in the absolute Idea nor, in relative identity with majesty, as a relation of servility in which individuality too would be something simply posited. On the contrary, in the Idea infinity is genuine; individuality as such is nothing and simply one with absolute ethical majesty—for which genuine, living, non-servile oneness is the only true ethical life of the individual.

We have accused scientific empiricism, so far as it is scientific, of the positive nullity and untruth of its principles, laws, etc., on the ground that it confers the negative absoluteness of the Concept on determinate features by means of the formal unity in which it places them, and it asserts them as existing positively, absolutely, and of themselves as end and destiny, principle, statute, duty, and law— forms that mean something absolute. But in order to acquire the unity of an organic relation which offers to this qualitative determination a mass of such concepts, one facet (expressed as end, destiny, or statute) must be given primacy over the other facets of the multiplicity, and these must be posited as unreal and null by comparison with it. It is in this process of application and consistent reasoning that perception as an inner totality is nullified. It is therefore by inconsistency that this assumption of facets into the Concept can be corrected and the violence done to perception undone, because inconsistency immediately cancels the absolute character previously conferred on one facet.

From this point of view, the old and thoroughly inconsistent empiricism must be justified, not in relation to absolute science as such, but in relation to the consistency of empirical scientific method, our subject so far. A great and pure intuition can in this way express the truly ethical in the purely architectonic method of its exposition, in which the context of necessity and the domination of form do not visibly appear. It is like a building which silently displays the spirit of its creator in its outspread mass, although the image of the creator himself, concentrated into a unity, is not exhibited there. In such an exposition, constructed with the help of concepts, it is due only to an unskilfulness of reason that it does not elevate into the ideal form what it comprises and penetrates, and does not become conscious of it therein as Idea. If perception will only remain true to itself and not let itself be confused by the understanding, it will be awkward as regards concepts which it needs to express itself; it will assume wrong shapes in its passage through consciousness; and will be both incoherent and self-contradictory concerning the Concept. But the ordering of the parts and self-modifying facets will betray the inner rational, though invisible, spirit; and in so far as the spirit's appearance here is regarded as product and result, the product will, as product, completely correspond with the Idea.

For the understanding, nothing is easier than to pounce on this empiricism, to pose other grounds against these unskilful ones, to express the confusion and contradiction of its concepts, to draw from separate propositions inferences which express the harshest and most irrational contradictions, and in all sorts of ways to display the unscientific character of empiricism. This serves empiricism right, especially if it either pretends to be scientific or adopts a polemical attitude to science as such. On the other hand, if specific characteristics are fixed, if their law is carried consistently through the aspects hunted up by empiricism, if intuition is made subordinate to them and if, in short, what is generally called a "theory" is framed, then empiricism is right to complain that this is one-sided; and it is in its power, by means of the completeness of the specific characteristics which it upholds, to force this theory (by citing instances) into a universality which is totally empty.

This restrictedness of concepts, the fixing of specific characteristics, the elevating of one selected aspect of appearance to universality and granting dominion over the others, has in recent years styled itself not just "theory," but "philosophy," and when it rose to emptier abstractions and seized on purer negations such as freedom, pure will, humanity, etc., styled itself "metaphysics." Believing that it has produced philosophical revolutions in natural law and especially in constitutional and criminal law, it has lugged these sciences hither and thither with such baseless abstractions and positively stated negations such as freedom, equality, the pure state, etc., or with equally baseless features drawn from common experience, like coercion—especially psychological coercion with its whole accompaniment of opposition between practical reason and natural impulses, and whatever else is at home in this psychology. And further, it has more or less consistently forced null concepts like these into the texture of a science in the guise of laws, rational ends, and rational principles.

Empiricism rightly demands that such a philosophy should take its bearings from experience. It rightly sticks to its obstinate opposition to such an artifical framework of principles. It rightly prefers its own empirical inconsistency (grounded on an intuition, however dim, of a whole) to the consistency of such philosophizing. It rightly prefers its own confusion—for instance, of ethical life, morality, legality or, in the more special case of punishment, of revenge, security of the state, reform, execution of a threat, deterrence, prevention, etc. (whether from the point of view of science or practical life)—to the absolute distinction of these different facets of one and the same intuition and the characterization of the whole of these qualities by a single one of them. It rightly claims that the theory, and this thing styling itself "philosophy" and "metaphysics," has no application and contradicts the necessities of practical life. This inapplicability would be better expressed by saying that in this theory and this philosophy there is nothing absolute, no reality, and no truth. Finally, empiricism rightly reproaches this philosophizing for its ingratitude on the ground that empiricism itself supplies it with the content of its concepts and then must watch this content being corrupted and perverted by philosophizing; for empiricism offers the specific character of the content entangled and bound up with other specific characters, and this specific character is essentially an organic and living whole, which is killed by this dismemberment and this elevation of unsubstantial abstractions and details to absoluteness.

If it were and remained pure itself, an empirical attitude would have every right to assert itself against such theorizing and philosophizing, and to treat the mass of principles, ends, laws, duties, and rights as not absolute but as distinctions important for the culture through which its own vision becomes clearer to it. But when empiricism seems to go to war with theory, it usually turns out that the one like the other is a vision already contaminated and superseded by reflection and a perverted reason. And what is alleged to be an empirical method is only weaker in abstraction and has been less self-sufficient in distinguishing and fixing its restricted concepts which it has not itself selected; on the contrary, it is entangled in such concepts as have become fixed in the culture of the day as "healthy common-sense" and so seem to have been drawn directly from experience. The picture of the struggle between such hardened and *ad hoc* conventionally fixed abstractions is necessarily just as checkered as the opponents themselves. Each uses against the other now an abstraction, now a so-called experience, and on both sides empiricism founders on empiricism, and narrowness on narrowness. Now principles and laws are boastfully advanced against philosophy, and philosophy is set aside as incompetent to judge of such absolute truths in which the understanding is stuck; now philosophy is misused for the purpose of ratiocination, in the name of philosophy.

This relative right which, when perception is its ruling element, was conceded to empiricism over against the mating of the empirical, and the product of reflection refers, as will be remembered, to its unconscious inner nature. But the middle term between this inner nature and its external appearance (i.e., consciousness) is the point where its insufficiency (that is, its one-sidedness) lies. And its drive against the scientific and incomplete connectedness, and its mere brush with the Concept whereby it is only contaminated, arises from the necessity that multiplicity and finitude be absolutely engulfed in infinity or universality.

We now turn to consider *infinity*, the principle of the *a priorism* which opposes itself to empiricism.

The manner in which empiricism arrives at its views and in them mixes up the complex with the simple, contrary to the Concept, is in the absolute Concept or infinity purged of its vacillation, and the incomplete separation of the two is made total. On a lower plane of abstraction, infinity, regarded as the absoluteness of the subject, is stressed in Eudaemonism generally, and it is stressed in the particular field of natural law by the systems which are called antisocialistic and posit the being of the individual as the primary and supreme thing; but infinity is not raised there to the pure abstraction which it has received in the idealism of Kant and Fichte.

This is not the place to expound the nature of infinity and its multiple metamorphoses, because, since it is the principle of movement and change, its essence is nothing but to be the unmediated opposite of itself. In other words, it is the negatively absolute, the abstraction of form which, as pure identity, is immediately pure non-identity or absolute opposition which, as pure ideality, is with equal immediacy pure reality; as the infinite, is the absolutely finite; as the indeterminate, is absolute determinacy. That absolute transition into its contradictory, which is its essence, and the disappearance of every reality into its opposite can be checked in no way other than by proceeding empirically, fixing one of the two aspects (i.e., reality or the subsistence of the opposites) and abstracting from the contradictory, the nullity of this subsistence. This real opposition pits complex being or finitude against infinity as the negation of multiplicity and, positively, as pure unity; the absolute Concept thus constituted provides in this unity what has been called "pure reason." But once more the relation of this pure unity to the multiplicity of beings standing over against it is itself a double relationship, either the positive relation of the existence of both or else the cancellation of both. However, this existence and this cancellation are both to be understood as only partial, for were the existence of the two absolute, they could not be related at all, while if the complete cancellation of both were settled, there would be no existence of either. This partial existence and partial negation of both—"the opposition of a divisible ego to a divisible non-ego in the ego" (i.e., in the relation which just for this reason is a partial one)—is the absolute principle of this philosophy.°
In the former positive relation the pure unity is called theoretical reason, in the negative relation, practical reason. And since in the latter relation the negation of the opposition is primary, and hence the unity is more subsistent, while in the former relation the maintenance of the opposition is primary and hence multiplicity is primary and more subsistent; therefore practical reason appears here as real, and theroretical reason as ideal.
But it is plain that this character belongs wholly in the sphere of

---

° [Fichte: *Grundlage der gesammten Wissenschaftslehre*, Part I, §3].

opposition and appearance. For the pure unity, posited as reason, is of course negative and ideal if what is opposed to it, the many (here the irrational), simply subsists—just as it appears more subsistent and more real when the many are posited as negated, or rather as [something] to be negated. But this irrational many, since nature is posited in opposition to reason as pure unity, is irrational only because it is posited as the non-substantial abstraction of the many while reason is posited as the non-substantial abstraction of the one. But, regarded in itself, the many is just as much absolute unity of the one and the many, as unity is. And nature or theoretical reason, which is the many, must, as absolute unity of the one and many, be characterized conversely as real reason. The ethical reason, however, which is unity (as absolute unity of the one and the many), must be characterized as ideal reason because in the opposition reality is on the side of multiplicity while ideality is on the side of unity.

Thus, in what is called practical reason, we can recognize only the *formal* Ideal of the identity of the real and the ideal, and in these systems of philosophy this Idea should be the absolute point of indifference. But this Idea does not arise from difference, and the ideal does not attain reality, for although the ideal and the real are identical in this practical reason, the real remains flatly opposed [to the ideal]. This real is essentially posited outside reason, and practical reason resides only in its difference from it. The essence of this practical reason is understood as a causal relation to the many—as an identity that is absolutely infected with a difference and does not go beyond appearance. This science of ethics, ° which talks of the absolute identity of ideal and real, belies its own words; its ethical reason is, in its essence and in truth, a non-identity of ideal and real.

Ethical reason was characterized just now as the absolute in the form of unity, and thus, since it is posited as something determinate it seems immediately in this determination to be posited just as essentially with an opposite. But the distinction is that true reality and the absolute in this regard are wholly free from this opposition

---

° [Probably a reference to Fichte: *System der Sittenlehre*, e.g., §18.]

to nature and are the absolute identity of ideal and real. The Absolute is known, according to its Idea, as this identity of differents whose determinate character is to be unity in the one case and multiplicity in the other. And this determinate character is ideal, i.e., it exists only in infinity according to the Concept expounded above; it is as much superseded as posited. Each of them, the unity and the multiplicity, whose identity is the Absolute, is itself a unity of one and many. But the unity whose ideal determinate character is multiplicity is the persistence of the opposites (i.e., positive reality), and therefore is necessarily an opposed and double relation. Since the real subsists in it, its identity is a relative one, and this relative identity of the opposites is necessity. Since this identity is thus in difference, its relation itself or the identity of the relation must be something different; it is also necessary that both unity and multiplicity be primary in it. This double relation determines the twofold aspect of the necessity, or the appearance, of the Absolute.

Since this twofold relation applies to multiplicity, and provided we term "indifference" the unity of the differents which stand on the other side and in which that reality or the many is superseded, then the Absolute is the unity of indifference and relation. And since the relation is double, the appearance of the Absolute is determined (i) as the unity of indifference and of the relation, or the relative identity, in which the many is primary and the positive, and (ii) as the unity of indifference and of that relation in which the unity is primary and the positive. The former is physical nature, the latter ethical nature. And since indifference or unity is freedom, while the relation or the relative identity is necessity, therefore each of these two appearances is the oneness and indifference of freedom and necessity. Substance is absolute and infinite; this predicate "infinity" implies the necessity of the divine nature or its appearance, and this necessity finds its expression as reality precisely in a double relation. Each of the two attributes itself expresses substance and is absolute and infinite, or the unity of difference and relation. And in the relation, the unity's indifference is so posited that the many is primary in the relation of the ones, while in the relation of the others, the one is primary, or the thing that sweeps onto the others. But since unity is primary in ethical nature, even in its relation, therefore ethical nature is free in this relative identity (i.e., in its necessity). Or, since the relative identity is not superseded because the unity is primary, this second freedom is so determined that the necessary *is* for ethical nature, but is posited negatively.

Now if we were to isolate this aspect of the relative identity of ethical nature, and to recognize the absolute unity of indifference and this relative identity—not as the essence of ethical nature, but as the aspect of relation or of necessity—then we would stand at the same point at which the essence of practical reason is characterized as possessing absolute causality, or as being free, and necessity as being only negative but for that very reason still posited. As a result, this very freedom does not escape from difference; relation or relative identity is made the essence, and the Absolute is conceived solely as negatively absolute or as infinity.

The empirical and popular expression whereby this notion, which conceives ethical nature purely under the aspect of its relative identity, has won such wide acceptance, is (i) that the real, under the name of sensuousness, inclinations, lower appetites, etc. (moment of the multiplicity of the relation), and reason (moment of the pure unity of the relation) do not correspond, this non-correspondence being the moment of the opposition of unity and multiplicity; and (ii) that reason consists in willing out of its own absolute self-activity and autonomy, and in constricting and dominating that sensuousness (moment of so determining the relation that in it unity or the negation of multiplicity is primary). The reality of this notion is grounded on the empirical consciousness and on the universal experience of discovering within oneself both that duality and also this pure unity of practical reason or the abstraction of the ego.

There is no question of denying this standpoint; on the contrary, it has been characterized above as the aspect of the relative identity of the being of the infinite in the finite. But this at least must be maintained, that it is not the absolute standpoint in which the relation has been demonstrated and proved to be only one aspect, and the isolation of the relation is likewise thus proved to be something one-sided. It must be maintained that, since morality is something absolute, this is not the standpoint of morality and there is no morality in it. And as for the appeal to ordinary consciousness, it must just as necessarily include morality as that standpoint which is the principle of immorality, since relation, isolated for itself, is posited as being in itself and not as a moment. Empirical consciousness is empirical simply because the moments of the Absolute appear in it dispersed, side by side, one after another, scattered; but it would be no ordinary consciousness if morality did not occur in it this way. This formal philosophy could choose amongst these diverse appearances of the moral and immoral which occur in empirical consciousness. Philosophy, not ordinary consciousness, is at fault for having chosen the appearance of the immoral, and for having imagined that it had the true absolute in the negative absolute or in infinity.

The construction of this practical philosophy rests on the presentation of what this negative absoluteness can achieve, and we must trace the chief features of the false attempt to exhibit a true absolute in the negative absolute.

It is obvious at once that, since pure unity constitutes the essence of practical reason, it is so completely out of the question to speak of a system of morality that not even a plurality of laws is possible. For what goes beyond the pure concept, or—since this pure concept (in so far as it is posited as negating the many, i.e., as practical) is duty— for what goes beyond the pure concept of duty and beyond the abstraction of a law, no longer belongs to this pure reason. Kant, the man who has expounded this abstraction of the concept in its absolute purity, recognizes full well that practical reason totally renounces the content of law and can do nothing beyond making the *form* of *fitness* of the will's (*Willkühr*) maxim into supreme law. The maxim of the arbitrary will (*Willkühr*) in choosing has a content and includes a specific action, but the pure will (*Wille*) is free from specification. The absolute law of practical reason is to elevate that specification into the form of pure unity, and the expression of this specification taken up into this form is the law. If the specification can be taken up into the form of the pure Concept, if it is not cancelled thereby, then it is justified and has itself become absolute through negative absoluteness as law and right or duty.

But the content of the maxim remains what it is, a specification or singularity, and the universality conferred on it by its reception into the form is thus a merely analytic unity. And when the unity conferred on it is expressed in a sentence purely as it is, that sentence is analytic and tautological. And the production of tautologies is in truth what the sublime lawgiving power of pure practical reason's autonomy in legislating consits of. The pure identity of the Understanding, expressed in theoretical terms as the principle of contradiction, remains exactly the same when it is turned to the practical form. When the question: "What is truth?" is put to logic, and answered by logic, it affords to Kant "the ludricrous spectacle of one man milking a he-goat and another holding a sieve beneath." The question: "What is right and duty?" put to and answered by pure practical reason is in the same position. Kant sees that "a universal criterion of truth must be such as would be valid of any and every knowledge regardless of the difference between its objects, but that, since using the criterion is abstracting from the whole content of knowledge, while truth concerns just this content, it is clearly quite impossible and absurd to ask for a general test of the truth of such content,"° since the test is also supposed not to concern the content of knowledge. In saying this, Kant is pronouncing judgment on the principle of duty and right set up by practical reason. For practical reason is the complete abstraction from all content of the will (*Wille*); to introduce a content is to establish a heteronomy of choice (*Willkühr*). But what is precisely of interest is to know *what* right and duty are. We ask for the content of the moral law, and this content alone concerns us. But the essence of pure will and pure practical reason is to be abstracted from all content. Thus it is a self-contradiction to seek in this absolute practical reason a moral legislation which would have to have a content, since the essence of this reason is to have none.

If this formalism is to be able to promulgate a law, some matter, something specific, must be posited to constitute the content of the law. And the form given to this specific matter is unity or universality. "That a maxim of thy will shall count at the same time as a principle of universal legislation" †—this basic law of pure practical

---

° [Both quotations are from *K.d.r.V.*, A 58.]

† [*K.d.p.V.*, Book I, ch. 1, §7.]

reason expresses the fact that something specific, constituting the content of the maxim of the particular will, shall be posited as concept, as universal. But every specific matter is capable of being clothed with the form of the concept and posited as a quality; there is nothing whatever which cannot in this way be made into a moral law. Every specific matter, however, is inherently particular, not universal; the opposite specific thing stands over against it, and it is specific only because there is this specific opposition. Both are equally capable of being thought; which of the two is to be taken up into the unity or to be thought, and which is to be abstracted from, is completely open and free. If the one is fixed as absolutely subsistent, then, to be sure, the other cannot be posited. But this other can just as easily be thought and, since the form of thinking is the essence, expressed as an absolute moral law.

"That the commonest untutored understanding can" engage in this easy operation and "distinguish what form of maxim is or is not adapted for universal legislation," Kant shows by an example: I ask whether my maxim to increase my fortune by any and all safe means can hold good as a universal practical law in the case where [appropriating] a deposit entrusted to me has appeared to be such a means; the content of this law would be that "anyone may deny having received a deposit for which there is no proof." This question is then decided by itself, "because such a principle as a law would destroy itself since the result would be that no deposits would exist." * But where is the contradiction if there were no deposits? The non-existence of deposits would contradict other specific things, just as the possibility of deposits fits together with other necessary specific things and thereby will itself be necessary. But other ends and material grounds are not to be invoked; it is the immediate form of the concept which is to settle the rightness of adopting either one specific matter or the other. For the form, however, one of the opposed specifics is just as valid as the other; each can be conceived as a quality, and this conception can be expressed as a law.

If the specification of property in general be posited, then we can

---

* [The quotations are from Kant: *K.d.p.V.*, Book 1, ch. 1 §4, Remark.]

construct the tautological statement: property is property and nothing else. And this tautological production is the legislation of this practical reason; property, if property *is*, must be property. But if we posit the opposite thing, negation of property, then the legislation of this same practical reason produces the tautology: non-property is non-property. If property is not to be, then whatever claims to be property must be cancelled. But the aim is precisely to prove that property must be; the sole thing at issue is what lies outside the capacity of this practical legislation of pure reason, namely to decide which of the opposed specific things must be lawful. But pure reason demands that this shall have been done beforehand, and that one of the opposed specific things shall be presupposed, and only then can pure reason perform its now superfluous legislating.

But the analytic unity and tautology of practical reason is not only superfluous but, in its expression or exercise it is false and must be recognized as the principle of immorality. The mere act of taking a specific thing up into the form of unity is supposed to alter the character of that thing's being. The specific thing, which by its nature has another specific thing over against it, the one being the negation of the other and neither therefore being absolute (and, so far as the functioning of practical reason goes, it does not matter which is which, for practical reason affords nothing but empty form), is thus supposed by this union with the form of pure unity to become absolute, to become law and duty. But when a specific and individual thing is elevated to something inherently [necessary], absurdity and, in the moral sphere, immorality are posited.

This transformation of the conditioned and unreal into something unconditioned and absolute is easily recognized in its illegitimacy and easily caught in its underhanded means. When the specific concept is expressed in a sentence, the specific thing, taken up into the form of pure unity or formal identity, produces the tautology of the formal sentence: the specific A is the specific A. The form, or in the sentence the identity of subject and predicate, is something absolute, but only negative or formal, and the specific A is unaffected; for the form, this content is something wholly hypothetical. However, the absoluteness, which by virtue of the sentence's form is

in the sentence, acquires a totally different meaning in practical reason. Absoluteness is also conferred on the content which by its nature is something conditioned; and this conditioned non-absolute, contrary to its own essence, is elevated into an absolute by this confusion. Producing a tautology is not the aim of practice, and practical reason would not take so much trouble for the sake of this idle form, which yet is all that is in its power. But by confusing absolute form with conditioned matter, the absoluteness of the form is imperceptibly smuggled into the unreal and conditioned character of the content; and in this perversion and trickery lies the nerve of pure reason's practical legislation. There is smuggled into the sentence "property is property," not its proper meaning, (i.e., "the identity which the sentence expresses in its *form* is absolute"), but the meaning: "the *matter* of the sentence (i.e., property) is absolute." And in this way anything specific can be made into a duty. The arbitrary will (*Willkühr*) has a choice between opposed specific things; and it would only be due to imcompetence if for any given action some ground could not be found which acquires not just the form of a *probable* ground, as with the Jesuits,° but the form of right and duty. This moral formalism does not exceed the moral skill of the Jesuits or, what coincides therewith, the principles of Eudaemonism.

It is well to note in this connection that adoption of the specific thing into the concept is understood in the sense that this adoption is something formal or that the specific thing is supposed to remain, so that matter and form contradict one another, the first being delimited and the second infinite. But if the content were really equated with the form and the specific thing with the unity, then no practical legislation would occur, but only the annihilation of the specific. Thus property itself is directly opposed to universality; equated with it, it is superseded.

This annihilation of the specific, through its adoption into infinity and universality, is indeed an immediate difficulty for practical legislation. For if the specific thing is such that in itself it

---

° [See Hegel: *Philosophy of Right* §140, and notes *ad. loc.* in Eng. tr. by T. M. Knox.]

expresses the supersession of something specific, then, by the elevation of the supersession to universality or to the state of having been superseded, not only the specific thing which is to be superseded, but the superseding itself, is cancelled. Thus a maxim referring to such a specific thing, which cancels itself when it is universalized, would not be capable of being the principle of a universal legislation, and so would be immoral. Alternatively, the maxim's content, which is the supersession of a specific thing, contradicts itself when it is raised to the concept. If the specific is thought as superseded, its supersession falls away; or else, if this specific is supposed to remain, then in turn the supersession laid down in the maxim is not laid down. Thus whether the specific remains or not, in either case its supersession is impossible. But a maxim which is in principle immoral, because self-contradictory, is absolutely rational and so absolutely moral because it expresses the supersession of a specific thing; for the rational in its negative aspect is the indifference of specifications, the supersession of the conditioned. Thus the specific injunction, "Help the poor," expresses the supersession of the specific thing, poverty. The maxim, "Help the poor," tested by being elevated into a principle of universal legislation, will prove to be false because it annihilates itself. If the thought is that the poor generally should be helped, then either there are no poor left or there are nothing but poor; in the latter event no one is left to help them. In both cases the help disappears. Thus the maxim, universalized, cancels itself. On the other hand, if the specific thing which is to be superseded (i.e., poverty) were to remain, the possibility of help remains—but only as a possibility, not as the actuality envisaged by the maxim. If poverty is to remain in order that the duty of helping the poor can be fulfilled, this maintenance of poverty forthwith means that the duty is not fulfilled. So the maxim of honorably defending one's country against its enemies, like an infinite number of other maxims, is self-cancelling as soon as it is thought as a principle of universal legislation; for when so universalized, for example, the specification of country, enemies, and defense is cancelled.

Unity does not have the purely negative meaning of the mere cancellation of specific things; nor is it the true unity of perception or

the positive indifference of these specifications. A comparison with this latter unity will clarify the perverted essence of the former in another aspect. That unity of practical reason, namely, is essentially affected with a difference because it is defined either as the fixing of one specific thing, whereby others are immediately excluded (posited negatively), or as an analytic sentence, in which case the identity of the sentence, its form, forthwith contradicts its content. In other words, as a sentence with its content, the analytic sentence contradicts the requirement that the sentence be a judgment. The sentence was supposed to say something, but a tautological sentence says nothing, for it is not a judgment, because the relation of subject to predicate is purely formal and no difference between them is posited. Alternatively, if the unity is taken as universality, then it refers entirely to an empirical multiplicity, and the present specification will be opposed to an endless throng that are empirically different. On the other hand, the unity of perception is the indifference of the specifications which make up a whole; it is not the fixing of them, as separate and opposed, but their summation and objectification. Since this indifference and the different specifications are plainly united, this unity of perception is not a cleavage between indifference as possibility and the differents as actualities; not a cleavage between the differents, some as possible and others as actual. All are actually present in it. And in this force of perception and presentness lies the force of morality in general, and naturally also of morality in particular with which this legislating reason is primarily concerned, and from which that form of the concept, of formal unity and universality, must rather be kept entirely separate. For this form is precisely what directly cancels the essence of morality, since it makes the morally necessary into something contingent by causing morality to appear in opposition to other matters; in morality, however, contingency, which coincides with the empirically necessary, is immoral.

A pain is lifted by the force of perception from feeling, where it is something accidental and contingent, into unity and the shape of something objective and absolutely necessary. By this immediate unity, which does not trouble at all about the possibilities which formal unity entails, it is maintained in its absolute presentness.

Owing, however, to the objectivity of perception and the elevation of independent being into this unity, it is genuinely severed from the subject and made ideal in the fixed perception of this unity. On the other hand, when compared by the unity of reflection with other specifications, or considered and rejected as a universal, this pain is in either case made contingent; as a result, the subject knows himself purely in his contingency and particularity, which knowledge is the sentimentality and the immorality of impotence. Alternatively, if morality bears on relations between individuals, it is pure perception and ideality (e.g., in the entrusting of a deposit) which has to be maintained and preserved from the interference of formal unity and the thought of the possibility of other specific features. The expression of that unity of perception, "a property of someone else entrusted to me is the property of someone else entrusted to me, and nothing else," has a totally different meaning from the tautology, expressed in universal terms, of practical legislation: "Another's property entrusted to me is another's property entrusted to me." For the latter sentence may equally well be confronted by this other: "What is not another's property entrusted to me is not the property of the other;" this means that a specific feature elevated into the concept is thereby made ideal, and its opposite specific feature may be posited just as easily. On the other hand, the expression of perception contains a *this*, a living relation and absolute presentness, with which the possibility is itself absolutely linked, and whereby a possibility separated therefrom, or a "being other," is absolutely annihilated, because in such a possible "being other" lies immorality.

Now if the unity of practical reason were not this positive unity of perception, but had only the negative meaning of annihilating anything specific, it would then simply express the essence of negative reason or of infinity, or the absolute Concept. But because this infinity is fixed and sundered from the absolute, it shows itself in its essence to be its own opposite. It mocks reflection, which wishes to hold it fast and to grasp in it an absolute unity by producing the opposite of this unity as well, a difference and multiplicity, (in the midst of this clash which is reproduced *ad infinitum* by permitting only a relative identity, whereby even as infinity it is the opposite of itself), namely absolute finitude. And by being so

441

isolated, it is itself only the powerless form, forsaken by the truly annihilating might of reason—the form which takes in specifications and harbors them within itself, not annihilating them but on the contrary perpetuating them.

On the opposition which has been expounded, on the fixing of it as a reality and its incomplete colligation as a relative identity, there hangs the recent definition of the concept of natural law and its relation to the whole science of ethics. Hitherto our analysis has been in general terms; we must now consider in more detail how the separation, insuperable once made, appears in its own special way in the science of natural law.

The absolute Concept, which is the principle of opposition and also opposition itself, shows itself (because it is fixed) in the separation so that, as pure unity opposed to itself, it is multiplicity; so that, it remains absolute Concept both under the form of pure unity and under that of pure multiplicity; so that in the form of multiplicity it is not a variety of different specific concepts, but is subsumed under multiplicity just as under unity. The Concept subsumes *itself* in many specific concepts, and is not a many but a one. The absolute Concept (itself a multiplicity) is a number of subjects to which it is opposed, in the form of pure unity, as absolute quantity, against this its own qualitative posited existence. Thus are posited (i) an inner oneness of the opposites, which is the essence of both, is the absolute Concept; and (ii) a severance of this Concept under the form of unity, in which form it is right and duty, and under the form of multiplicity, in which it is a thinking and willing subject.

The former aspect—under which the essence of right and duty, and the essence of the thinking and willing subject, are one and the same—is (as is, in general, the higher abstraction of infinity) the great element in the philosophy of Kant and Fichte. But that philosophy has not remained true to this oneness; by recognizing this oneness as the essence and the absolute, it posits the separation into the one and the many just as absolutely, and places one beside the other as equals. As a result, the oneness is not the positive Absolute which has constituted the essence of both and in which they would be one, but the negative Absolute or the absolute Concept. And further, this necessary oneness becomes formal; the two opposed specifications, posited absolutely, thereby in their subsistence fall under ideality, which is to this extent the pure possibility of both. It is possible for right and duty to have reality independently as something particular apart from individuals, and for individuals to have reality apart from right and duty; but it is also possible that both are linked together. And it is absolutely necessary for both possibilities to be separate and to be kept distinct, so that each may ground a special science—one dealing with the unity of the pure concept and the subjects, or the morality of actions, the other with their non-unity, or legality—in such a way that, if in this division of the ethical sphere into morality and legality, the two become mere possibilities, they both are equally positive for that very reason. Of course the one is negative for the other; but so they both are. It is not that one is the absolutely positive, the other the absolutely negative; each is both in their relation to one another, and since at first both are only relatively positive, neither legality nor morality is absolutely positive or genuinely ethical. And since each of them is just as positive as the other, both are absolutely necessary; and the possibility that the pure concept and the subject of right and duty are *not* one must be posited unalterably and without qualification.

Hence the fundamental concepts of the system of legality reveal themselves directly as follows. There is a conditioning of pure self-consciousness. This pure self-consciousness, the ego, is the true essence and the absolute, but nevertheless it is conditioned, and its condition is that it advances to a real consciousness; These two forms of consciousness remain downright opposed to one another in this relation of being mutually conditioned. That pure self-consciousness, pure unity, or the empty ethical law (the universal freedom of everyone) is opposed to real consciousness; i.e., to the subject, to the rational being, to individual freedom. Fichte expresses the matter in a more popular way as the presupposition that "faith and constancy are lost." * On this presupposition a system is built whereby both the concept and the individual subject of ethical life are supposed to be united despite their separation,

---

* [Fichte, *Grundlage des Naturrechts*, § 14]

though the unity is on this account only formal and external, and this relation between them is called "compulsion." In this way the external character of oneness is utterly fixed and posited as something absolute and inherently necessary; and thereby the inner life, the rebuilding of the lost constancy and faith, the union of universal and individual freedom, and ethical life itself, are made impossible.

Here we confine ourselves to Fichte's argument. It is the most consistent and the least formal, and it really is an attempt at a consistent system which would have no need of the religion and ethics that are foreign to it. In a system of such an externality, as in any argument that proceeds from conditioned to conditioned, nothing unconditioned can be exhibited; or if it is posited, it is only formal indifference which has the conditioned differents outside itself, essence without form, power without wisdom, quantity without inner quality or infinity, rest without movement.

The supreme task in an "arrangement working with mechanical necessity," * the task of compelling the activity of every individual to accord with the general will—since this general will must necessarily be real in the subjects who are its organs and administrators—is a task which presupposes an opposition between the individual will and the general will. Oneness with the general will thus cannot be understood and posited as inner absolute majesty, but only as something which is to be brought about by an external relation or by compulsion. But in reality, in the process of compulsion and supervision which is to be set going, there can be neither an infinite series nor a leap from the real to the ideal. There must be a supreme positive point from which compulsion according to the concept of universal freedom starts. But this point, like all others, must be compelled to compel according to the concept of universal freedom; a point which in this universal system of compulsion would not be compelled would depart from the principle [of the system] and be transcendent. Now the question is how this supreme will, by compulsion and supervision, is also to become correspondent with the concept of the general will, and

---

* [Ibid.]

how the system is accordingly to remain wholly immanent and transcendental. This could happen only if the power of the whole were so distributed between the two sides that stand over against one another that the governed are compelled by the government, and *vice versa*. If the power and, with it, the possible compulsion by either side is given unequal strength, then the result is that—in proportion as one part has more power than the other, or as each has an excess over the other—only one part, and not its opposite, is under compulsion, which ought not to happen. But, strictly speaking, only excess power is truly powerful, because in order for something to set limits to something else it must be equal to it. The weaker is no limit for the stronger; both must thus compel and be compelled reciprocally with equal power.

But if in this way action and reaction, position and opposition, are equally strong, the power on both sides is reduced to equilibrium, and all activity, action, and expression of the will is thereby cancelled. The reduction [of the opposites] may be thought either positively or negatively: action and reaction may be posited as existing and working, or they may be posited negatively; and equilibrium results from the fact that there is neither action nor reaction. Nor is it a true solution to propose a remedy for this death by extending the immediate confrontation [of the opposites] into a circle of effects and so apparently cancelling the mid-point of their contact (where the reduction of the opposites appears) by the deceptive expedient of leaving this mid-point empty. Against the hierarchy of compulsion descending from the supreme power through all its branches down to every individual, a similar pyramid is in turn supposed to rise upwards from the individuals to the supreme pinnacle of counterpressure meeting the descending pressure. Thus the whole is supposed to bend in a circle wherein the immediacy of contact would vanish, the forces insofar as they are massed together would be held apart, and intervening members would produce that artificial difference. Thus no member reacts directly on that by which it is moved (producing equilibrium), but always on some other member, so that the first moves the last and the last the first. But such a *perpetuum mobile* whose parts are all supposed to follow one another round the circle, will, instead of moving, settle at once into complete equilibrium and become a complete *perpetuum quietum*; for pressure and counterpressure, coercing and being coerced, are entirely equal, and they stand directly against each other and effect the same reduction of forces as in the first conception. Pure quantity cannot be deceived by such mediation whereby no difference whatever, no true infinity or form, is introduced into it; it remains as before a completely undivided pure formless might. On this line, might cannot be compelled to fit the concept of universal freedom, for there is no power outside it, and no division can be set up within it.

The next thing, therefore, is a resort to a purely formal distinction. *Actual* power is of course posited as one, united in the government; but it is opposed by possible power, and this possibility, it is claimed, can as such compel that actuality. This second powerless existence of the general will is supposedly entitled to judge whether the power has forsaken the first kind of will to which it is tied, or whether the power no longer fits the concept of universal freedom. The general will is supposed to supervise the supreme power generally and, when a private will replaces the general will in it, to wrest that power from this private will. This is supposed to happen by way of a public declaration, with absolute authority, of the total nullity of every action of the supreme power of the state from this moment onwards. It would be insurrection for this power to separate itself by its own independent decision. But this must not happen since this pure power consists entirely of private wills which, accordingly, are incapable of constituting themselves as a general will. But it is this second general will which declares this mass of private wills to be united as a community, or the pure power to be united with the Idea of the general will, because the latter no longer exists in the former holders of power.

Whatever institution is posited to wring something from the supreme power, this institution must be invested with, not the mere possibility of, but power itself. But since this power is held by the other representatives of the general will, it can hinder any such institution, and nullify whatever functions are given to the

Ephorate°—supervision, public declaration of the interdict, and whatever other formalities are hatched. And all this is done with as much right as those in whose hands the operation of this institution would have been placed. For these Ephors are also just as much private wills as the others are; and whether their private will has sundered itself from the general will is a matter that the government can judge just as easily as the Ephorate can judge the government. The government, moreover, can enforce its judgment. It is known that on the occasion of a government's recent dissolution of a rival and paralyzing legislative force, a man who was himself involved in it (responding to the suggestion that the establishment of a supervisory commission similar to Fichte's Ephorate would have prevented such an atrocity) judged correctly that a council with similar supervisory powers and the will to oppose the government would have been treated just as violently.

Lastly, however, if the holders of supreme power decided of their own volition to permit this second representative of the general will to summon the community to choose between them and the supervisors—what would be set in motion with such a mob, who would also supervise all private matters, whose life is even less public, and who is simply not educated to be conscious of the general will, or to act in the spirit of the whole, but exactly the opposite?

What this has shown is that the ethical order posited according to relations alone, or externality and coercion understood as a totality, is self-cancelling. This proves indeed that coercion is nothing real, nothing in itself. This will become even clearer if we show it in relation to coercion itself according to its concept and according to the specific character which the relation of this tie has. For, in part, dialectic has to prove that relation is nothing whatever in itself, and, in part, this has already been briefly shown above.

Of the concepts in general which go together with coercion and express precisely this relation, it has been shown in part above that they are abstractions without substance, *entia rationis*, or creatures of imagination, without reality. First, there appears the empty

---

°[Fichte, *Grundlage des Naturrechts*, §16.]

abstraction of the concept of the universal freedom of all, separate from the freedom of individuals; and next, on the other side, this very freedom of the individual, comparably isolated. Each, posited by itself, is an abstraction without reality; but both, as absolutely identical and then posited merely *in* this first fundamental identity, are something quite different from those concepts which have their significance only in non-identity. Next, natural or original freedom is to be limited by the concept of universal freedom. But that original freedom, which may be posited as limitable, is for this very reason nothing absolute. And further, it is an inherent contradiction to construct an idea that the freedom of the individual, through the externality of coercion, is with absolute necessity adequate to the concept of universal freedom. This is simply to imagine that the individual, by means of something not absolute, is yet absolutely equal to the universal. In the concept of coercion itself, something external to freedom is immediately posited. But a freedom for which something is genuinely external and alien is no freedom; its essence and its formal definition is just that nothing is absolutely external.

We must completely reject that view of freedom whereby freedom is supposedly a choice between opposed entities, so that if +A and −A are given, freedom consists in selecting *either* +A *or* −A and is absolutely bound to this *either-or*. Anything like this possibility of choice is wholly an empirical freedom which is one with empirical common necessity, and wholly inseparable from it. Freedom is rather the negation or ideality of the opposites, as much of +A as of −A, the abstraction of the possibility that neither of them *is*. Something external would *be* for freedom only if freedom were characterized as only +A or only−A. But freedom is just the opposite; nothing is external for it, so that for it no coercion is possible.

Everything specific is in its essence either +A or −A; and −A is indissolubly linked to +A, just as +A is to −A. As soon as the individual has put himself in the specific position +A, he is equally tied to −A, and −A is something external for him, not in his power. On the other hand, because of the absolute tie between +A and −A, he would be brought directly under the alien power of −A because of the specific position of +A. And a freedom, which is supposed to consist in choosing to determine itself as either +A or −A, would never escape from necessity. When freedom determines itself as +A it has not annihilated −A; rather, −A subsists quite necessarily as something external for it; and the same is true *vice versa* if it determines itself as −A. Freedom is freedom only if it (positively or negatively) unites −A and +A and so ceases to determine itself as +A. In the union of these two specific positions both are annihilated: +A−A=0. If this nought is understood purely relatively to +A and −A, and the indifferent A itself is understood as something specific (a plus or a minus in contrast with another minus or plus) absolute freedom is beyond this opposition, just as it is above any opposition and any externality, and is simply insusceptible of any coercion; and coercion has no reality whatever.

But this idea of freedom seems itself to be an abstraction; and if, for example, we were talking of concrete freedom, that of the individual, then this would establish that existence of a specific object, and thereby establish purely empirical freedom as a possibility of choice—and thus also empirical necessity and the possibility of coercion, or in general the opposition of universality and singularity. For the individual is singularity, and freedom is the annihilation of singularity: in virtue of singularity the individual is directly under specific [limitations]; thus something external is there for him, and coercion is therefore possible. But it is one thing to put specific limitations on the individual, under the form of infinity, and another to put them on him absolutely. Specific limitation under the form of infinity is also cancelled thereby, and the individual *is* only as a free being; i.e., since specific determinations are posited in him he is the absolute indifference of these determinations, and in this his ethical nature formally consists. So too, individuals generally being different, whether from themselves or from something other, and having a bearing on something external, this externality itself is indifferent and a living relation (i.e., organization), and herein, since totality occurs only in an orgainzation, consists the positive element in ethical life.

But the indifference of the single individual is a negative one in relation to the being of the specific determinations. But when his

447

being is posited as individuality (i.e., as a negation positively insuperable for his being, as a specific determination whereby the external as such is held fast), then what remains to him is only purely *negative* absoluteness, or infinity: the absolute negation of both +A and −A, or the absolute adoption of this individual being into the concept. Since −A is something external to the subject's determination +A, this relation places the subject under an alien power. But since he can with equal facility posit his +A negatively as a determination, and can cancel and alienate it, he remains perfectly free in the face of the possibility or the actuality of an alien power. By negating +A as well as −A, he is subdued but not coerced. He would have to suffer coercion only if +A were absolutely fixed in him, which would allow an endless chain of other determinations to be attached to the man who is himself a determination. The possibility of abstracting from determinations is without restriction; in other words, there is no determination which is absolute, for this would be a direct self-contradiction. But freedom itself (or infinity) is indeed the negative and yet the absolute, and the subject's individual being is absolute singularity taken up into the concept, is negatively absolute infinity, pure freedom. This negatively absolute, pure freedom, appears as death; and by his ability to die the subject proves himself free and entirely above all coercion. Death is the absolute subjugator. Because the subjection is absolute, or because in it individuality becomes pure individuality and not the positing of +A with the exclusion of −A (an exclusion which would be no true negation but only the positing of −A as something external and of +A simultaneously as a determination), but the cancellation of the plus and minus alike, the individuality is therefore its own concept, and so infinite. And the opposite of itself, or absolute liberation, and the pure individuality which is in death, is its own opposite, universality. Thus there is freedom in subjection because subjection bears purely on the cancellation of a determination, not simply one side of the determination, but the determination posited positively as well as negatively, subjectively as well as objectively; and so, considered in itself, freedom keeps itself purely negative. Or, since the cancelling can itself be grasped and expressed positively by reflection, the cancellation of both sides of the determination appears accordingly as the completely equal positing of the determined on both its sides.

Applied to punishment, for example, this means that retribution alone is rational in it; for by retribution the crime is subjugated. A state of affairs +A brought about by the crime is complemented by the bringing about of −A, and so both are annihilated. Or, looked at positively, with the state of affairs +A there is linked for the criminal the opposite state −A, and both are brought about equally, while the crime had brought about one only. Thus the punishment is the restoration of freedom, and the criminal has remained, or rather been made, free, just as the punisher has acted rationally and freely. In this, its specific character, punishment is thus something in itself truly infinite and absolute, revered and feared on its own account. It issues from freedom, and, even as subjugator, remains in freedom. If, on the other hand, punishment is understood as coercion, it is posited merely as a specific determination and as something purely finite, carrying no rationality in itself. It falls wholly under the common concept of one specific thing contrasted with another, or as an item with which something else—the crime—can be purchased. The state as judicial power trades in specific wares, called crimes, for sale in exchange for other specific wares [punishments], and the legal code is its price-list.

But however null this abstraction and the relation of externality arising from it may be, the moment of the negatively absolute or infinity (which is indicated in this example as determining the relation of crime and punishment) is a moment of the Absolute itself and must be exhibited in *absolute ethical life*. We shall take the versatility of absolute form or of infinity in its necessary moments, and show how they determine the shape of absolute ethical life; this will lead us to the true concept and relation of the practical sciences. Since the point here at present is to characterize the relations involved in these moments, and since the aspect of infinity must thus be emphasized, we presuppose the positive principle that the absolute ethical totality is nothing other than a *people*, a point that will also be demonstrated in the following moments of the negative which we are considering here.

In absolute ethical life, infinity—or form as the absolutely negative—is nothing other than subjugating, as understood above, taken up into its absolute concept. There it relates not to single specific matters, but to their entire actuality and possibility, that is, to life itself. Thus matter equals infinite form, but in such a way that its positive element is the absolutely ethical element (i.e., membership in a people); the individual proves his unity with the people unmistakeably through the danger of death alone. Through the absolute identity of the infinite, or of the aspect of relation, with the positive, ethical totalities, such as peoples, take form and constitute themselves as individuals; and thus, peoples, as individuals, take their position against individual peoples. This position and individuality are aspects of reality. Understood otherwise, they are mere *entia rationis;* it would be a case of an abstract essence without absolute form, an essence that is therefore essenceless. This bearing of individuality on individuality is a relation, and therefore is twofold: (i) the positive bearing of one on the other, the calm and even co-existence of both side by side in peace; (ii) the negative bearing (i.e., exclusion of one by the other); and both are absolutely necessary. As for the second, we have conceived the rational relation as a subjugation taken up into its concept, or as the absolutely formal virtue of courage. This second aspect of the bearing which the shape and individuality of one ethical totality has on another is what establishes the necessity of war. In war there is the free possibility that not only certain individual things but the whole of them, as life, will be annihilated and destroyed for the Absolute itself or for the people; and therefore war preserves the ethical health of peoples in their indifference to specific institutions, preserves it from habituation to such institutions and their hardening. Just as the blowing of the winds preserves the sea from the foulness which would result from a continual calm, so also corruption would result for peoples under continual or indeed "perpetual" peace.

Since the shape of ethical totality and its individuality is fixed as an individuality facing outwards, and the movement of this individuality is fixed as courage, the negative side of infinity, which has just been considered, is immediately bound up with the other side, namely the persistence of the opposition. One side is infinity, negative like the other; the first is negation of negation, opposition against opposition; the second is negation and opposition even in its persistence as specific characteristics or manifold reality. These realities in their pure inner formlessness and simplicity (i.e., these feelings) are in the practical sphere feelings which reconstruct themselves out of difference and, passing from the cancellation of undifferentiated self-awareness, are restored through an annihilation of perceptions. These are physical needs and enjoyments which, put again on their own account in a totality, obey in their infinite intertwining one single necessity and the system of universal mutual dependence in relation to physical needs and work and the amassing [of wealth] for these needs. And this system, as a science, is the system of the so-called political economy. Since this system of reality rests entirely on negativity and infinity, it follows for its relation to the positive totality that it must be treated wholly negatively by the latter, and must remain subject to the domination of this relation. Whatever is by nature negative must remain negative and may not become fixed. In order to prevent this system from becoming a self-constituting and independent power, it is not enough to set up the propositions that every one has a right to live, that in a people the commonweal has to see to it that every citizen shall have a sufficiency, and that there be perfect security and ease of gain. This last proposition, understood as an absolute principle, would on the contrary exclude a negative treatment of the system of possession, and would allow the system full sway to entrench itself absolutely. But the ethical whole must on the contrary preserve in this sytem the awareness of its inner nullity, and impede both its burgeoning in point of quantity, and the development of ever greater difference and inequality for which its nature strives. In every state a process goes on more or less unconsciously in the shape of an external natural necessity from which it would have wished to be exempt. With the growth of the system of property, the expenditure of the state increases continually and taxes rise proportionately. This reduces possession and makes acquisition more difficult, especially through war, which introduces many-sided confusion into the business of acquisition, as well as jealousy of other classes and restraint of trade, sometimes with consent, sometimes, through ignorance etc., without it. The result is that things go on to such a degree that the positive ethical life of the state itself permits the purely real [economic] system to become independent [of the individual] and the negative and restricting attitude to be upheld.

Reality, in the context in which it has just been considered and of which some different aspects are physical necessity, enjoyment, possession, and the objects of possession and enjoyment, is pure reality. It simply expresses the extremes of the relation. But the relation also contains an ideality, a relative identity of the opposed determinacies; thus, this identity cannot be positively absolute but only formal. Through the identity into which the real aspect of the context of the relations is posited, possession becomes property, and particularity in general, even living particularity, is simultaneously determined as universal, and thus the sphere of law is constituted.

As for the reflection of the Absolute in this relation, it has already been characterized above in its negative aspect as a subjugation, opposed to the persistence of the real and delimited. In its positive aspect, for the persistence of the real, the indifference in this delimited material can express itself only as an external and formal equality. The science relating to this subject can only aim at determining the degrees of inequality and, to make this possible, at determining how something living or internal can be made so objective and external that it is amenable to this determination and assessment. The absolute reality of ethical life is, at this stage,* restricted to this superficial appearance owing to the persistence of the reality present in the opposite. The equating and calculating of inequality not only has its limits, owing to the fixed determination which implies an absolute opposition, and, like geometry, encounters incommensurability, but—since it remains wholly in determinacy and yet cannot abstract, as geometry can; but, being involved in living relationships, is always confronted by whole

---

* [*Potenz*. This word, adopted from the vocabulary of mathematics by Schelling, means "power." "Stage" is used to translate it here, becasue it is clear later that agriculture, etc., are *Potenzen* within a system of law; i.e., not merely "sphere" but stages also.]

bundles of such determinacies—it also encounters endless contradictions. This contradiction among determinacies is of course remedied and disposed of, in the case of pure perception, by fixing and clinging to single determinacies, whereby a decision can be made, and this is always better than no decision at all. For, since there is nothing absolute in the matter itself, the essential thing after all is the formal principle that some decision and settlement be made. But it is quite a different thing for a decision to be made in accordance with true total justice and ethical life. The fixing and absolute clinging to determinacies makes such justice impossible, or possible only by confusing these. True total justice is actual only in immediate ethical perception which subjugates the determinacies posited as absolute, and seizes only the whole.°

Plato, speaking in his plain language about the two sides, (i) the endless determining of the infinite reception of qualities into the concept, and (ii) the contradiction of their individuality in face of perception and therefore amongst themselves, says: "It is clear that the art of legislation belongs to the art of kingship. But the best thing is that the man who is wise and kingly, and not the laws, should rule, ... because the law could not completely prescribe with precision what would be most excellent and most just for everybody always. This is because the dissimilarities of men and actions and the perpetual restlessness, so to say, of human affairs make it impossible for any art at all to lay down for all time any simple rule applicable to all cases of anything. . . . But we see the law aiming at almost this uniformity, like an obstinate and ignorant man who lets nothing happen contrary to his order and allows no one to question his order even if something new and better, though against his order, turns up for some individual. . . . Thus it cannot be a good thing to apply a universally simple rule to what is never simple." †

The persistence of the notion that, in this sphere of human affairs, inherently absolute and specific law and duty are possible results from the formal indifference, or the negative absolute, which has its place and is indeed implicit only in the fixed reality of this sphere.

°[That is, direct moral perception grasps justice as a whole; it supersedes determinate traditional rights, and restores social harmony.]

† *Politicus*, 294.

But as implicit it is empty; in other words, there is nothing absolute in it except just pure abstraction, the utterly vacuous thought of unity. It is not an inference from a preceding experience, nor can it be regarded as an accidental incompleteness of the concrete or of the realization of an *a priori* true idea. On the contrary, we must recognize that what is here called "idea," and the hope for a better future based on that idea, is inherently null and void, and that perfect legislation is inherently impossible, just as true justice, corresponding to the determinacy of the law, is impossible *in concreto* (in the exercise of the power of jurisdiction). As for the former inherent impossibility, the Absolute, supposedly appearing in the specifications as such, is only the infinite. The very same empirical infinity and inherently endless determinability posited here is posited in the notion of comparing a specific measure with an absolutely indeterminate line, or of a specific line with an absolutely indeterminate measure, or the notion of measuring an infinite line or absolutely dividing a determinate line. As for the latter concrete impossibility, each of the views (equally as infinite in number and infinitely different in shape) that constitute the object of jurisdiction is defined ever more variously as the legal definitions grow in number. This development of distinctions through legislation renders every individual view more distinguishable and more developed, and the expansion of legislation does not mean an approximation to the goal, a positive perfection which here, as was shown above, has no truth; it is no more than the formal aspect of the growing development. And now, in order that the One, the judicial view of law and judgment, may become organized and a genuine unity and whole within this multiplicity, it is absolutely necessary that every single one of the specifications of law be modified (i.e., be partly cancelled precisely as an absolute, self-existent specification of that for which it claims to be the law), and hence, that its absoluteness be not respected. Nor can there by any question of pure application, for pure application would be the establishment of some single specifications to the exclusion of others. But these others, in virtue of existing, demand that they be taken into account, so that the reciprocal effect, determined not by parts but by the whole, may itself be a whole. This clear and determinate knowledge must rest on the empty hope and the formal concept both of an absolute legislation and of a jurisdiction exempt from the inner [conviction] of the judge.

Our treatment of the system of reality has shown that absolute ethical life must take a negative attitude to that system. The Absolute, as it appears under the system's fixed determinacy, is ·posited in it as a negative absolute, as infinity which presents itself as a formal, relative, and abstract unity contrasting with the opposition. In the former negative attitude it is hostile to the system; in the latter, it is under its dominion; in neither is it indifferent to it.° Yet that unity which is the indifference of opposites (and which cancels and encompasses them within itself) and that unity which is only formal indifference or the identity of the relation between subsisting realities, must themselves just be as one through the complete absorption of the relation into indifference itself. This means that the absolute ethical order must organize itself completely as shape, since relation is the abstraction of the aspect of shape. Though becoming wholly indifferent in the shape, the relation does not lose its nature of relation. It remains a relation of organic to inorganic nature.

But, as was shown above, the relation as an aspect of infinity is itself something duplex: in one regard the ideal, and in the other the many or the real, is primary and predominant. In the first regard, the relation is, strictly speaking, in the shape and in indifference; and the eternal restlessness of the concept or of infinity is in part in the organization itself, self-consuming and surrendering the purely quantitative and the appearance of life, in order that it might rise eternally, its own seed-corn, from its ashes to new youth. And in part, it eternally cancels its outward difference, and, feeding on and producing the inorganic, it calls forth from indifference a difference or relation to an inorganic nature, and in turn cancels that relation and consumes that nature as it consumes itself. We will soon see what this inorganic nature of the ethical is. But, secondly, in this aspect of relation or infinity it is also posited that what has been

---

° [As the ideal, the Absolute transcends what really exists; it judges it and is hostile or negative in its attitude towards it. But in so far as the Absolute is embodied in the real world it is subordinate to it, and its attitude has to be one of positive acceptance.]

cancelled endures; for, precisely because the absolute concept is its own opposite, the being of difference is posited along with its pure unity and negativity. In other words, the cancelling posits something that it cancels, the real; and so there would be an actuality and difference which ethical life cannot surmount. Individuality, which (in virtue of the residence which infinity has taken up in the whole strength of its opposition, not just *in potentia* but *in actu*) is actually in opposition, could not cleanse itself from the difference and absorb itself into absolute indifference. That both the supersession of the opposition and its subsistence are not just ideal but also real is in general the positing of a separation and elimination, so that reality, in which ethical life is objective, would be divided into one part which is absorbed absolutely into indifference, and another wherein the real as such subsists and thus is relatively identical, and carries in itself only the reflection of absolute ethical life.

Thus there is posited a relation of absolute ethical life, which would reside entirely within individuals and be their essence, to relative ethical life which is equally real in individuals. Ethical organization can remain pure in the real world only if the negative is prevented from spreading all through it, and is kept to *one* side. We have shown above how indifference appears in prevailing reality and is formal ethical life. The concept of this sphere is the real *practical* realm; on the subjective side, feeling or physical necessity and enjoyment; on the objective side, work and possession. And this practical realm, as it can occur according to its concept (assumed into indifference), is the formal unity or the *law* possible in it. Above these two is the third, the Absolute or the ethical. But the reality of the sphere of relative unity, or of the practical and legal, is constituted in the system of the latter's totality as a class of its own.

Thus, two classes are formed in accordance with the absolute necessity of the ethical. One is the class of the free, the individual of absolute ethical life; its organs are the single individuals. Regarded in respect of its indifference, it is the absolute living spirit, and in respect of its objectivitity it is the living movement and the Divine self-enjoyment of this whole in its organs and members, the totality of the individuals. But its formal or negative side must again be the absolute one (i.e., work) which proceeds not to the nullifying of single determinations, but to death; and its product, too, is not something singular but the being and preservation of the entirety of the ethical organization. The task that Aristotle assigns to this class is what the Greeks called πολιτεύειν, which means living in and with and for one's people, leading a general life wholly devoted to the public interest—or else the task of philosophizing.° Plato, in keeping with his higher sense of life, wants these two tasks not to be separated but wholly linked together.†

The other class consists of those who are not free; it exists in the difference of need and work, and in the law and justice of possession and property; its work concerns the individual and thus does not include the danger of death. To these two we must add the third class: in the crudity of its uneducative work, it deals only with the earth as an element, and its work has the entirety of need before it in its immediate object without intermediaries, and thus itself is a genuine totality and indifference like an element. Thus it lacks the difference of the understanding characteristic of the second class. It maintains the bodies of its members and its spirit in the possibility of formal, absolute ethical life, or of courage [the virtue of the first class], and of a violent death; and, hence, it can add the force of its numbers and their elemental being to the first class.

These two classes exempt the first from the relation in which reality in respect of their inaction or action is fixed as possession and property and as work, just in the same way as the class of earners, like a specializing species amongst modern nations, has in our time gradually ceased to do military service, and courage has constituted itself in a purer manner into a special class exempted by those others from acquisition, a class to which both possession and property are at best accidental. The constitution of this second class is in its substance characterized by Plato as follows: the art of kingship "exterminates by death and punishes by exile and the greatest of disgrace those who have no share of courage or temperance or any other virtuous inclination, and by the necessity of an evil nature are violently carried away to godlessness, arrogance, and in-

---

° [*Politics*, 1255 b, 35–37.]

† [*Republic*, 473.]

justice, . . . but those who are wallowing in ignorance and baseness are reduced to the class of slaves under the yoke." ° And Aristotle discerns what is consonant therewith: "He who is by nature not his but another man's is a slave . . . . as body is related to spirit." †

But the relation of this man, who by nature is another's and has not his spirit in himself, to absolutely independent individuality may be something twofold in form: either a relation of the individuals of this class as particulars, to the individuals of the first class as particulars, or a relation of universal to universal. In the empirical phenomenon of the universality of the Roman Empire, that former relation of slavery vanished of itself. With the loss of absolute ethical life and the degradation of the class of the nobility, the two formerly separate classes became equals; and, with the loss of freedom, slavery ceased of necessity. When the principle of formal unity and equality had to be imposed, it generally cancelled the inner true difference of the classes. At first, that principle did not succeed in bringing about the above-mentioned separation of classes, still less the form of separation which they conditioned. In accordance with this form these classes are, under the form of universality, in the relation of domination and dependence only as whole class to whole class, so that even in this relation the two in their bearing on one another remain universal; while in the relation of slavery the form of particularity determines the relation. Here it is not class against class; on the contrary this unity of each single part [in a whole] is dissolved in the real bearing [of one on the other], and individuals are dependent on individuals. The principle of universality and equality first had so to master the whole that instead of separating the classes it amalgamated them. In this amalgam, under the law of formal unity, the first class is in truth entirely cancelled, and the second alone becomes the people, a change depicted by Gibbon in these terms: "This long peace, and the uniform government of the Romans, introduced a slow and secret poison into the vitals of the empire. The minds of men were gradually reduced to the same level, the fire of genius was extinguished, and even the military spirit

---

° *Politicus*, 308-9.
† *Politics*, 1254 a-b.

evaporated. . . . Personal valour remained, but they no longer possessed that public courage which is nourished by the love of independence, the sense of national honour, the presence of danger, and the habit of command. They received laws and governors from the will of their sovereign . . . . The posterity of their boldest leaders was contented with the rank of citizens and subjects. The most aspiring spirits resorted to . . . the standard of the emperors; and the deserted provinces, deprived of political strength or union, insensibly sunk into the languid indifference of private life." °

This universal private life, and the situation in which the nation consists solely of a second class, immediately establishes the formal legal relationship which fixes, and posits absolutely, individual separate existence. And indeed, the most complete structure of a system of law based on this relationship has formed and evolved out of such corruption and universal degradation. This system of property and law which, owing to this fixation of individuality, consists not in anything absolute and eternal, but wholly in the finite; and the formal must constitute itself in a class of its own, and in that case must be able to expand in its whole length and breadth, really separate and isolated from the class of the nobility. To this system belong not only the in themselves subordinate and purely formal questions about the legal basis of property, contract, etc., but also, in general, the whole endless expansion of legislation to cover matters listed and specified thus by Plato: "These subjects of legal contracts that one man makes with another about things or workmen; actions for abuse or assault; legal declarations, impannelling of juries; collection and payment of dues in markets or harbors; . . . all of them are things on which it would be unworthy to dictate to good men. They will easily discover for themselves the many things that have to be laid down about these matters . . . if God grants them secure possession of a truly ethical constitution. Otherwise they will pass their lives multiplying petty laws and amending them, thinking that at last they will reach perfection . . . . They live like invalids who from intemperance will not give up their bad diet. . . . By all their remedies they achieve nothing except engendering and

---

° [Ed. J. B. Bury, (London, 1925), 1:56–57.]

multiplying greater diseases, while always hoping that someone will advise a drug to make them better. . . . Equally charming are those who make laws on matters like those mentioned and constantly amend them in the belief that they will reach finality—unaware that in fact they are just cutting off a Hydra's head."[*]

"Now it is true that with increasing licentiousness and disease in a city many lawcourts are opened . . . and no greater proof of a bad and disgraceful discipline can be found than when excellent doctors and judges are needed not only by bad men and artisans, but also by those who claim to have been brought up in a free system . . . and who are compelled to have recourse to a justice laid on them by others as masters and judges and spend a lot of time in pleas and defences in court."[†] This system has to develop at the same time as a universal state of affairs, and has to destroy free ethical life wherever the latter is mixed up with those relationships—and not from the start kept separate from them and their consequences. Thus it is necessary that this system be consciously adopted, recognized in its rightfulness, excluded from the class of the nobility, and be given a class of its own for its realm, where it can make itself secure and develop its whole activity in its own muddle and the superseding of one muddle by another.

Accordingly the scope of this class is characterized by the facts that its sphere is possession generally and the justice possible here in matters of possession, that it also makes up a cohesive system, and that, as an immediate consequence of the fact that the relation of possession is taken up into formal unity, each individual, being as such capable of possession, is related to all others (the community) as being a burgher in the sense of a *bourgeois*. For the political nullity resulting from the fact that the members of this class are private individuals, the burgher finds compensation in the fruits of the system; i.e., peace and gain and perfect security in their enjoyment individually and as a whole. The individual's security as a whole is involved because he is exempt from courage and spared the necessity (laid on the first class) of exposing himself to the danger of violent death—a danger which means for the individual the absolute

[*] *Republic*, 425c–426e.
[†] Ibid., 405a-b.

insecurity of all enjoyment, possession, and law. As a result of the supersession of this confusion of principles, and their established and conscious separation, each of them is done justice, and that alone which ought to be is brought into existence (i.e., the reality of ethical life as absolute indifference, and at the same time the reality of that indifference as real relation in persistent opposition) so that the second is overcome by the first and this compulsion itself is made identical and reconciled. This reconciliation lies precisely in the knowledge of necessity, and in the right which ethical life concedes to its inorganic nature, and to the subterranean powers by making over and sacrificing to them one part of itself. For the force of the sacrifice lies in facing and objectifying the involvement with the inorganic. This involvement is dissolved by being faced; the inorganic is separated and, recognized for what it is, is itself taken up into indifference while the living, by placing into the inorganic what it knows to be a part of itself and surrendering it to death, has all at once recognized the right of the inorganic and cleansed itself of it.

This is nothing else but the performance, on the ethical plane, of the tragedy which the Absolute eternally enacts with itself, by eternally giving birth to itself into objectivity, submitting in this objective form to suffering and death, and rising from its ashes into glory. The Divine in its form and objectivity is immediately double-natured, and its life is the absolute unity of these natures. But the movement of the absolute contradiction between these two natures presents itself in the Divine nature (which in this movement has comprehended itself) as courage, whereby the first nature frees itself from the death inherent in the other conflicting nature. Yet through this liberation it gives its own life, since that life *is* only in connection with this other life, and yet just as absolutely is resurrected out of it, since in this death (as the sacrifice of the second nature), death is mastered. But, appearing in the other nature, the Divine movement so presents itself that the pure abstraction of this nature, which were a purely infernal, purely negative power, is cancelled through living unification with the Divine nature. It so presents itself that the Divine casts its light into this nature and through this ideal unity in spirit makes it into its reconciled and living body; and this body, as body, remains in difference and evanescence, and, through the spirit, beholds the Divine as something alien.

The picture of this tragedy, defined more particularly for the ethical realm, is the issue of that litigation between the Eumenides (as powers of the law in the sphere of difference) and Apollo (the god of indifferenced light) over Orestes, conducted before the organized ethical order, the people of Athens.* In the human mode, Athens, as the Areopagus, puts equal votes in the urn for each litigant and recognizes their co-existence; though it does not thereby compose the conflict or settle the relation between the powers or their bearing on one another. But in the Divine mode, as Athene, Athens wholly restores to the people the man [Orestes] who had been involved in difference by the god [Apollo] himself; and through the separation of the powers both of which had their interest in the criminal, it brings about a reconciliation in such a way that the Eumenides would be revered by this people as Divine powers, and would now have their place in the city, so that their savage nature would enjoy (from the altar erected to them in the city below) the sight of Athene enthroned on high on the Acropolis, and thereby be pacified.

Tragedy consists in this, that ethical nature segregates its inorganic nature (in order not to become embroiled in it), as a fate, and places it outside itself; and by acknowledging this fate in the struggle against it, ethical nature is reconciled with the Divine being as the unity of both. To continue this metaphor, *Comedy*, on the other hand, will generally come down on the side of absence of fate. Either it falls within absolute vitality, and thus presents only shadows of clashes (or mock battles with a fabricated fate and fictitious enemies), or else it falls within non-life and therefore presents only shadows of self-determination and absoluteness; the former is the old, or Divine, comedy, the latter the modern comedy.

Dante's *Divine Comedy* is without fate and without a genuine struggle, because absolute confidence and assurance of the reality of the Absolute exist in it without opposition, and whatever opposition

---

*[The reference is to the play of Aeschylus, *The Eumenides*.]

brings movement into this perfect security and calm is merely opposition without seriousness or inner truth. This opposition may present itself—over against the divinity which seems alien and external, though resting in absolute certainty—as the residue or dream of a consciousness of individual self-sufficiency, or as a consciousness of selfhood which, though fixed and firmly held, is totally impotent and without force. Or else the opposition may present itself in a divinity, sensed in the self and aware of itself, which consciously makes up its own conflicts and games in which, with absolute frivolity, it sets some of its members to a given prize and carries its various aspects and features to their full term in perfect individuality, causing them to develop into organizations of their own. Indeed it cannot as a whole take its movements to be movements against a fate, but only to be chance events, because it regards itself as invincible, counts loss as nothing, and is certain of its absolute dominion over every singularity and wantonness, aware, as Plato said in another connection, that a "πόλις [city] is amazingly strong by nature."° Such an ethical organization will thus, for example, without risk of fear or envy, drive individual members on to the highest exercise of talent in every art and science and skill, and make them into something particular there, certain within itself that such divine monstrosities of beauty do not impair its own shape but are comic traits which brighten one feature of that shape. As such gay intensifications of individual traits we may regard, to cite one people only, Homer, Pindar, Aeschylus, Sophocles, Plato, Aristophanes, and others. But both in the serious reaction against the ever more seriously developing individuality of Socrates, and still more in the regret and shame because of it, and in the pullulating abundance and high energy of the individualizations that were burgeoning at the same time, we must not fail to discern that [the city's] inner vitality had thereby announced that it was going to its extremes, that it proclaimed its strength in the maturity of these seeds but also the approaching death of this body which bore the seeds. And thus the city had to accept the conflicts—which she generally provoked, and which she could incite and carry on as

---

° [*Politicus*, 302 a.]

chance events with equal frivolity, even in their more serious and extensive forms, such as wars—no longer as mere shadows but as a fate soon to be overpowering.

Elsewhere belongs that *other comedy* whose complications are without fate and without true struggle, because ethical nature itself is caught in that fate. Here the climax is reached in conflicts that are not playful but serious for this ethical urge, though comical for the spectator. And rescue from them is sought in an affectation of character and absoluteness which is contantly deceived and dethroned. The ethical urge (for it is not the conscious absolute ethical nature which plays a part in this comedy) must, to put it briefly, transmute the existent into the formal and negative absoluteness of law. And thereby it must give its anxious mind the impression that its possessions are secure, must lift all its belongings to safety and certainty by contracts and all imaginable varieties of clause and subclause in the formulary. It must deduce appropriate systems from experience and reason, which are certainty and necessity itself, and base them on the most acute ratiocination. But just as, in the poem,* the souls in hell saw all the plants they had planted in the deserts of hell swept away by the next gale, the ethical urge here must similarly witness how the next change or even the ascent of the earth-spirit wipes out half, or entire, sciences proved by experience and reason; how one legal system overthrows another; how humaneness here displaces severity, while elsewhere the will to power takes the place of the security of contract; and how in science, as in reality, the most securely acquired and confirmed possessions of principles and laws are ravaged and destroyed. The ethical urge must either think that these are its own efforts, hovering above fate with reason and will, which work themselves out in such matters and have produced such changes; or it must get perturbed by their unexpected and inappropriate character, and first call on all the gods for help against this necessity, and then truckle under to it. In both cases the ethical urge, which seeks an absolute infinity in these finite things, merely performs the farce of its faith and its undying illusion (which is darkest where it is brightest), it being already lost and in the wrong

---

*[Klopstock: *Messiah*, ii. 370–387. Pöggeler's note.]

when it imagines itself to be resting in the arms of justice, trustworthiness, and pleasure.

The comedy so separates the two zones of the ethical that it allows each to proceed entirely on its own, so that in the one the conflicts and the finite are shadows without substance, while in the other the Absolute is an illusion. But the true and absolute relation is that the one really does illumine the other; each has a living bearing on the other, and each is the other's serious fate. The absolute relation, then, is set forth in tragedy.

For although, in the living shape or organic totality of ethical life, that which constitutes the real side of that life is in the finite, and therefore cannot fully take up the bodily essence of the finite into the divinity of that life; it nevertheless expresses in itself the absolute Idea of divinity, though in a distorted way. Ethical life, to be sure, does not inwardly unite into absolute infinity the moments of this Idea that are kept separate as necessity; on the contrary, it has this unity only as a counterfeit negative independence—i.e., as freedom of the individual. But yet this real essence is utterly bound up with the absolute indifferent nature and shape of ethical life. While it must look upon that nature as something *alien,* it nonetheless *looks* on it and is in spirit one with it. Even for that essence itself, the very first thing is that the absolutely pure and indifferent shape and the absolute ethical consciousness shall *be,* and the second thing is the irrelevancy that, as the real, this essence shall be related to that consciousness merely as its empirical consciousness; just as it is primary that an absolute work of art shall *be,* and it is only secondary whether this specific individual is its creator or only an onlooker who enjoys it. This existence of the Absolute is necessary, but equally necessary is this partition: i.e., on the one hand the living spirit, the absolute consciousness, and the absolute identity of the ideal and the real sides of ethical life itself shall harmonize; while on the other hand, the spirit's corporeal and mortal soul cannot in its empirical consciousness completely unify its absolute form with its inner essence. Nevertheless, this spirit enjoys a view of the Absolute, as it were, as alien. In its real consciousness, it is one with the Absolute through fear, trust, and obedience, while in its ideal consciousness it is wholly united with the Absolute in religion, the God of the community, and his service.

But what we have to put to one side, under the external form of the first class, is the real absolute consciousness of ethical life. It is consciousness and, as such (on its negative side), pure infinity and the supreme abstraction of freedom; i.e., the relation of coercion pushed to the point of cancellation, or freely chosen violent death. On the positive side, however, this consciousness is the singularity and separateness of the individual. But this inherent negativity (consciousness as such), of which the distinctions just made are merely its two aspects, is absolutely taken up into the positive; its separateness and infinity, or ideality, is absolutely and perfectly taken up into the universal and the real. This unity [of universal and particular] is the Idea of the absolute life of the ethical. In this oneness of infinity and reality in the ethical organization, the Divine nature—of which Plato says, "It is an immortal animal whose soul and body are eternally born together" °—seems to display the wealth of its multiplicity both in the highest energy of infinity and in unity which is the wholly simplex nature of the ideal element.

The most perfect mineral displays the nature of the whole in each part that is broken from a lump, but its ideal form is separateness, whether as the inner form of the fragment or the outer form of crystallization. This differs from the elements of water, fire, and air, where each particle is the perfect nature and representative of the whole, both in its essence and in its form or infinity. Moreover, the mineral's real form is not permeated with the true identity of infinity; its senses have no consciousness; its light is a single color, and cannot see; or if it is the indifference of colors, there is no point at which the passage of colors through it is impeded. It sounds when struck by some other object, but not of itself; its taste cannot taste; its smell cannot smell; its weight and hardness feels nothing. If it does not belong to the individuality of the characteristics of sense, but unites them in indifference, it is the undeveloped shut-in

---

° [Lasson suggests *Timaeus* 30b, but Pöggeler is surely right in referring to *Phaedrus*, 246d.]

absence of difference—not the unity which divides itself inwardly and subdues its division. So too, the elements which are the same in all their parts have in them only the possibility (not the actuality) of differences, and have indifference only in the form of quantity, not indifference in qualitative terms. But the earth as the organic and individual element extends through the system of that element's shapes, from primal rigidity and individuality into the qualitative sphere and difference. And only in the absolute indifference of ethical nature does it resume the complete equality of all its parts and the absolute oneness of the individual and the absolute—in the first aether° which, from its self-identical fluid and soft form, scatters its pure quantity through individual formations into individuality and number, and completely controls this absolutely brittle and rebellious system by the fact that number is purified to become pure unity and infinity, and becomes intelligence. Thus, by becoming absolutely negative, the negative can become perfectly one with the positively absolute; for the absolute Concept is its own absolute immediate opposite and, as one of the ancients says, "is nothing no less than it is something." † In intelligence the form or the ideal is absolute form, and real as such; and in the absolute ethical order absolute form is in the most genuinely possible way bound up with absolute substance. Of the individual formations that lie between simple substance in reality (as pure aether), and the marriage with absolute infinity, none can bring form and qualitative unity into absolute indifference with the essence and substance present in the ethical order (whether through the quantitative elemental equality of whole and parts or, in higher formations, through the individualization carried out in still more individual parts), or bring the formal unification of the parts into a whole by

---

° [*Aether*—primordial matter or absolute being, according to Hegel's *Jenenser Realphilosophie* (Leipzig, 1932), and to Schelling's philosophy of Nature, from which Hegel borrowed it.]

† [This may be an allusion to the discussion in Plato: *Sophist* 237–241, or (as Pöggeler suggests) to Aristotle: *Metaphysics* 985 ^{b}, 8–9, where this is said to be a doctrine of Leucippus.]

means of the fellowship of leaves in plants, of species, of the herd-wise life and common labor of animals. This is because in intelligence alone is individualization carried to the absolute extreme (i.e., to the absolute Concept), and there alone is the negative carried to the absolute negative; i.e., to being its own immediate opposite. Intelligence alone is thus capable (i) as absolute individuality, of being absolute universality, (ii) as absolute negation and subjectivity, of being absolute position and objectivity, and (iii) of being the supreme identity of reality and ideality, since it is absolute difference and infinity, absolute indifference, and the totality—*actu* in the unfolding of all clashes, *potentia* in their absolute annihilation and unification.

In the indifferences of light, the aether has scattered its absolute indifference into a multiplicity; in the blooms of the solar system it has born its inner reason and totality out into expansion. But the individualizations of light are dispersed in multiplicity, while those which form the orbiting petals of the solar system must maintain towards them a rigid individuality. And so the unity of the system lacks the form of universality, while the unity of the petals lacks pure unity, and neither carries in itself the absolute Concept as such. By contrast, in the system of the ethical order, the separately developed flowers of the heavenly system are closed; the absolute individuals are perfectly united into universality; reality, or the body, is supremely at one with the soul, because the real multiplicity of the body is itself nothing but abstract ideality, the absolute concepts of pure individuals; and thereby these latter can themselves be the absolute system. The Absolute is that which intuits itself as itself, and that absolute intuition and this self-knowing, that infinite expansion and this infinite recovery into itself, are simply one. But on this account, if both, as attributes, are real, spirit is higher than nature. For if nature is absolute self-intuition and the actuality of the infinitely differentiated mediation and unfolding, then spirit, which is absolute intuition of itself as itself (or absolute knowing), is, in the recovery of the universe into itself, both the scattered totality of this multiplicity, which it overarches, and the absolute ideality thereof in which it annihilates this separateness, and reflects it into itself as the unmediated point of unity of the infinite Concept.*

From this idea of the nature of absolute ethical life there arises a relationship still to be discussed: the relationship of the *individual's* ethical life to *real absolute* ethical life, and the relationship between the sciences thereof, namely morality and natural law. Since real absolute ethical life, united in itself, comprehends infinity (or the absolute Concept), pure individuality *sans phrase* and in its supreme abstraction, it is directly the ethical life of the individual. Conversely, the essence of the ethical life of the individual is *the* real and therefore universal absolute ethical life; the ethical life of the individual is one pulse beat of the whole system and is itself the whole system. We notice here too a linguistic allusion, elsewhere repudiated, which is fully justified by what has been said—namely that it is of the nature of absolute ethical life to be a universal or an *ethos*. This Greek word for ethical life, like the German one [*Sitte*], expresses this nature admirably, while the newer systems of ethics, in making independence and individuality into a principle, cannot fail to expose the relation of these words. This inner allusion proves so powerful that these systems, to define their subject-matter, could not misuse these words and so adopted the word "morality," which indeed originally meant the same thing, but, because it is rather only an invented word, does not quite as directly resist its inferior meaning. †

But, as has been shown, absolute ethical life is so essentially the ethical life of all that we can scarcely say of it that it mirrors itself as such in the individual. For it is of the essence of the individual, just as much as the aether which permeates nature is the inseparable

---

*[At this point Hegel's editors insert a space, but his essay appeared in two installments, and this is simply the point at which the first installment ended.]

†[In his later work, the *Philosophy of Right*, Hegel makes a clear distinction between *Sittlichkeit* and *Moralität*. These words are ordinarily snyonyms for "morality." But Hegel uses *Sittlichkeit* to mean conscientious abiding by the laws and customs or *ethos—Sitte—*of one's nation, and *Moralität* to mean conscientiousness simply. Thus a wrongdoer may be *moral* but not *sittlich*. English usage is different: a man may abide by the *mores* but not be moral. The translation of this essay usually renders *Sittlichkeit* by "ethical life" in accordance with the terminology of the *Philosophy of Right*, but "morality" is sometimes used where Hegel seems to be referring to individual, rather than social, behavior.]

essence of the configurations of nature, and, as space (the ideality of nature's appearances), is not separate at all in any of them. On the contrary, just as the lines and angles of the crystal (in which it expresses the external form of its nature) are negations, so too ethical life, in so far as it expresses itself in the individual as such, is something negative. *First,* it cannot express itself in the individual unless it is his soul, and this it is only in so far as it is a universal and the pure spirit of a people. The positive is prior by nature to the negative, or, as Aristotle says: "The state comes by nature before the individual; if the individual in isolation is not anything self-sufficient, he must be related to the whole state in one unity, just as other parts are to their whole. But a man incapable of communal life, or who is so self-sufficing that he does not need it, is no part of the state and must be either a beast or a god."°

Secondly, in so far as ethical life expresses itself in the individual as such, it is posited in the form of a negation; i.e., it is the possibility of the universal spirit. And the ethical qualities of the individual, such as courage or moderation or frugality or generosity, etc., are negative ethical life (i.e., in the particularity of the individual a singularity is not genuinely fixed and no real abstraction is genuinely made) and are possibilities or potentialities of being in universal ethical life. These virtues, which in themselves are potentialities and have a negative meaning, are the subject-matter of morality, and we now see that the relation of natural law to morality has in this fashion been reversed; I mean that morality properly deals only with the area of the inherently negative, while the true positive belongs to natural law as is implied in its name. Natural law is to construct how ethical nature attains its true right. If, on the other hand, the negative—both in itself and as the abstraction of externality, of the formal moral law, of the pure will, and the individual's will—and further, the syntheses of these abstractions (such as coercion, the limitation of individual freedom by the concept of universal freedom, etc.) were to express the specific character of natural law, it then would be a natural *wrong,* since on the basis of such negations as realities, ethical nature is thrown into utter corruption and misery.

° [*Politics,* 1253ᵃ, 25–29.]

But since these properties are the reflex of absolute ethical life in the individual as the negative (but the individual who is in absolute indifference with the universal and the whole), and so are its reflex in that life's pure consciousness, there must also be a reflex of them in that life's empirical consciousness, and this reflex must constitute the ethical nature of the second class, the one preoccupied with fixed reality, with possession and property and not with courage. Now this is the reflex which morality, in the usual meaning, would more or less fit—the *formal* positing, in mutual indifference, of the specific terms of the relation; i.e., the ethical life of the *bourgeois* or private individual for whom the difference of relations is fixed and who depends on them and is in them. A science of this morality is thus, first, a knowledge of these relations themselves, so that insofar as they are studied with reference to ethical life, a reference that can only be formal owing to their absolute fixity, the above-mentioned enunciation of tautology finds its place here: this relation is only this relation. If you are in this relation, then be in it with reference thereto; for if you perform actions bearing on this relation without acting with reference to it, you are annihilating the relation, cancelling it. At the same time, the true sense of this tautology directly implies that this relation itself is not absolute, and thus that morality too, which is dependent on it, is something contingent and not truly ethical. This true sense, according to what was said above, emerges from the fact that only the form of the concept, the analytic unity, is the absolute, and hence the negatively absolute, because the content, by being specific, contradicts the form.

But those properties(which are truly ethical, since in them the particular or the negative appears) taken purely into indifference may be called ethical properties. They may be called virtues only if they are individualized again to a higher power, and become like proper living shapes, though within absolute ethical life—such as the virtues of Epaminondas, Hannibal, Caesar, and some others. As powers of this kind, they are shapes, and thus are no more absolute themselves than the shapes of other organic formations. On the contrary, they are the stronger emergence of one aspect of the Idea of the whole. And the morals of virtues or ethics (if we wish to characterize the morals generally of morality and adopt the title of "ethics" to describe virtue) must therefore be exclusively a natural description of the virtues.

Now just as ethics has a bearing on the subjective or the negative, so a distinction must be made between the negative as the maintenance of difference and the negative as its absence. Hitherto the discussion has been about the former negative, but this other one, the absence of difference, presents the totality as something enclosed and not unfolded, where movement and infinity are not present in their reality. The living being under this form of the negative is the budding of ethical life, and *education* is by definition the emerging progressive cancellation of the negative or subjective; for the child, as the form of the potentiality of an ethical individual, is something subjective or negative, whose development to manhood is the cessation of this form and whose education is the disciplining or subjugation of the form. But the positive aspect and the essence of the child is that it is suckled at the breast of universal ethical life; it lives first in an absolute vision of that life as alien to it, but comprehends it more and more and so passes over into the universal spirit. It follows automatically that those virtues, as well as absolute ethical life, are not an effort to achieve a private and separate ethical life any more than is their development through education, and that it is vain and inherently impossible to strive after a private positive ethical life. As regards ethical life, the saying of the wisest men of antiquity is alone true, that "to be ethical is to live in accordance with the ethics of one's country." And as regards education, the reply of a Pythagorean° to the question: "What is the best education for my son?" is "Make him a citizen of a well-ordered state."

Thus the absolutely ethical has its own proper organic body in individuals, and its movement and vitality in the common being and doing of everyone is absolutely identical as both universal and particular. We have treated it in particularity, but in such a way that its essence is the absolutely identical, and thus, in general, have treated it in that identity. Therefore in the form of universality and knowledge too, it must present itself as a system of *legislation*, in

---

° [Xenophilus, according to Diogenes Laertius VIII. 1, ch. xv.]

such a way that this system completely expresses reality or the living customs present in the nation. This obviates what is often the case, namely that the laws of a nation fail to reveal what in that nation is right and realized. A lack of skill in formulating the true ethical principles as laws, and the fear of thinking these principles, of regarding them, as one's own, and acknowledging them, is the sign of barbarism. Yet this ideality of ethics and their form of universality in the laws must, insofar as it subsists as ideality, also be perfectly united with the form of particularity. In this way the ideality as such must be given a pure absolute shape, and so must be regarded and worshipped as the nation's God; and this view must in turn have its own vivacity and joyful movement in a cult.

We have now presented absolute ethical life, in the moments of its totality, and constructed its Idea. We have also done away with, as unsubstantial *entia rationis,* the prevailing distinction, in reference to ethical life, between legality and morality, and also the affiliated abstractions of the universal freedom of a formal practical reason. And we have specified—not at all by confusing both principles, but by cancelling them and constituting the absolute ethical identity— what the distinctions are between the science of natural law and of morals in accordance with the absolute Idea. Thus we have established that the essence of this Idea is not an abstraction but the living reality of the ethical, and that its difference concerns only the external and negative side. We have established that this difference is at the same time the completely reversed relation to the other difference, since according to the latter it is the formal and negative which is to be ascribed to natural law as its essence, and the absolute and positive to morality as *its* essence, yet such that even this absolute is in truth something no less formal and negative; and what is here called formal and negative is in the last resort simply nothing.

Now in order to expound the relation of *natural law* to the *positive sciences* of law, we only need to pick up its threads at the point where we left it and to indicate the place where it ends.

At the outset we note in general that philosophy arbitrarily sets its own limits in respect of a given science by means of the universality of the concept of a specific character or an element. A specific science is precisely the progressive presentation and analysis (in the higher sense of the word) of how that which philosophy leaves undeveloped as a simple specific character ramifies once more and is itself a totality. But the possibility of such a development lies *formally* in the fact that the law of absolute form and totality, by which a specification is to be further known and developed, is directly present in the Idea. But the *real* possibility is present in virtue of the fact that such a specific character or element, undeveloped by philosophy, is not an abstraction or a truly simple atom, but, like everything in philosophy, is reality; and a reality is reality because it is totality and itself the system of stages or elements. To display the element in this way is the development belonging to the specific science.

Consequently, we might say in advance that a good part and perhaps all of the sciences called positive jurisprudence would fall within a completely developed and elaborated philosophy, and that, by their constitution as sciences proper, they are neither excluded from philosophy nor opposed to it. Owing to the empirical distinction within this body of sciences and their independence, no true distinctions within the body are laid down by philosophy. No necessarily exclusive difference from philosophy is set up by the fact that they call themselves empirical sciences, some of which have their application in the actual world and propose to make their laws and procedure prevail in the eyes of the common way of conceiving things, while others bear on individual systems of existing constitutions and legislations and belong to a specific nation and time. For nothing needs to be so applicable and, in the eyes of the universal—the truly universal—way of conceiving things (for there are common ways which are very particular in this respect), needs to be so fully justified as what proceeds from philosophy, just as nothing needs to be so highly individual, living, and permanent as that. In order to discuss the relations of these sciences to philosophy, we must first establish and define a difference which makes them positive sciences.

In the *first* place, the positive sciences comprise, in the actuality on which they profess to have a bearing, not only historical matter but also concepts, principles, relations, and, in general, much which in itself belongs to reason and is supposed to express an inner truth and necessity. Now to invoke actuality and experience in favor of such matter, and to insist on them as something positive in contrast to philosophy, must be recognized as absolutely inadmissible. It is quite impossible that anything which philosophy has proved to be non-real should occur truly in experience. And if positive science invokes reality and experience, philosophy can declare its proof of the non-reality, even in its empirical bearing, of a concept upheld by positive science, and deny that the things that positive science claims to find in experience and actuality can indeed be found there. Philosophy will of course grant the notion that something is so experienced—a casual and subjective view. But when positive science claims to find and exhibit its ideas and basic concepts in experience, it means to assert something real, necessary, and objective—not a subjective view. Whether something is a subjective view or an objective idea, an opinion or a truth, philosophy alone can decide. It can leave to positive science its own method *ad hominem* and, besides denying that a scientific idea does in fact occur in experience, can maintain on the contrary that it is only a philosophic idea which is to be found in experience. Philosophy can exhibit its ideas in experience; the reason for this lies directly in the ambiguous nature of what is called experience. For it is not immediate intuition itself, but intuition raised into the intellectual sphere, thought out and explicated, deprived of its singularity, and expressed as a necessity, that counts as experience. Therefore the principal thing, in what is exhibited in and as experience, is not what (with reference to the cleavage introduced into intuition by thinking) we may call actuality. But when intuition is drawn into the sphere of thought, opinion must give way to the truth of philosophy. The distinction between what positive science assumes to have drawn directly from intuition (though thereby it has determined itself into being a relation and a concept of intuition), and what does not belong to thinking, is easily demonstrated in each case, as is the proof of philosophy's complete authority and mastery in the matter.

Secondly, thinking of this kind, which appeals to actuality, tends to be truly positive in its views, because it rests in opposition and holds on to specific details, and so takes *entia rationis* or *entia imaginationis* as absolute and derives its principles from them. Thus

472

it runs the risk of having every specific detail prove to it to be the opposite specific detail, and that from whatever it accepts, the very opposite is derived. For example, if the increased density or specific weight of a body is explained as an increase in the force of attraction, the same phenomenon can be explained with equal ease as an increase in the force of repulsion, for there can be only as much attraction as there is repulsion—the one has meaning only with reference to other. To the extent to which the one were greater than the other, to that same extent it would not exist at all. What is to be regarded as an increase in the one, can be considered as exactly an increase in its opposite.

Thus, in natural law generally, or in the theory of punishment in particular, a relation might be defined as coercion, though philosophy proves the nullity of this concept, and the positive science calls on experience and actuality to show that coercion is actually real, that coercion actually takes place. But the non-reality of this concept, proved by philosophy, can be asserted with just as much justice and with the appeal to experience and actuality—stating that there is no coercion, that no man has ever been coerced or ever will be. For here it all depends on how the phenomenon is explained, whether in support of the idea of coercion something is being considered as purely external or as something internal. Whenever the presence of coercion is to be demonstrated, the very opposite of one and the same phenomenon can be shown to be present (namely that it is not a coercion but rather an expression of freedom), for the phenomenon, by being taken in the form of idea and thus being determined by the inner and the ideal, leaves the subject in his freedom against coercion. And if, in order to remove the opposition of the internal and of freeom, what is supposedly external and coercion is itself transferred into the internal, so that psychological coercion is being asserted, this transfer of the outer into the inner is no help either. For thought remains free without qualification, and psychological or conceptual coercion cannot bind it. The possibility of cancelling the specific thing which is envisaged and is supposed to serve as coercion is absolute. It is perfectly possible that the loss of something specific, threatened by punishment, be accepted, and that what the law means to take forcibly by punishment be freely given up. Thus if the explanation of a phenomenon claims that the idea of something specific is or has been effective as coercion, the explanation on the opposite ground (that the phenomenon is an expression of freedom) is just as absolutely possible. The fact that the sensuous incentive (whether the one that supposedly prompts the action, or the one by which the law is supposed to deter from it) is psychological (i.e., something internal), at once places it in the sphere of freedom, freedom which could abstract from it or not— either of which is freedom of the will. If, on the other hand, it is held that we *suppose* that there is coercion (of a psychological sort) and that this is the common way of looking at things, this is, in the *first* place, not true; it is just as easy and doubtless more common to hold that an action or failure to act arises from free will. *Secondly,* in setting up principles and in making laws we would need to pay as little attention to opinion as astronomers, investigating the laws of the heavens, allow themselves to be hampered by the opinion that the sun, the planets, and all the stars revolve round the earth, and are just as big as they seem, etc.; and as little as the ship's captain bothers about the opinion that the ship is at rest and the shore is moving away. If those two were to accept those opinions, the astronomer would find it impossible to understand the solar system, while the captain would stop the oarsmen or lower the sails. Both would at once find it impossible to attain their objective and would be forthwith convinced of the unreality of the opinion at the moment they want to concede its reality. As was shown above, conceive coercion as reality (i.e., imagine it in a system and in the totality), and it at once annihilates itself and the whole.

Since such a specific detail, maintained by positive scientific opinion, is the very opposite of itself, it is equally possible for either of the two parties, holding one of the opposite details, to refute the other. This possibility of refutation consists in the fact that every specific detail can be shown to be neither thinkable, nor to exist at all, except in relation to its opposite. But because it exists and has meaning only in relation to the other, this opposite must directly exist and be shown just as much. If +A is meaningless except in relation to −A, it follows that, along with +A, −A is directly present.

The opponent now says that what is here is −A rather than +A; but the same reply can be made to his −A.

Often, however, we do not take even this much trouble. For instance, regarding *that* freedom which is opposed to sensuous incentives and which, because of this opposition, is no more a true freedom than they, we fail to show that everything proposed as its expression must in reality be explained as the effect of sensuous motives. This explanation can be made with ease; but with the same ease it can be shown, on the other hand, that what is supposed to be experienced as an effect of sensuous motives ought properly to be experienced as an effect of freedom. On the contrary we simply abstract from freedom and assert that freedom has no place here because it is something internal, nay more, something moral and indeed metaphysical. But no thought is given to the fact that the other specific detail at which we stop (i.e., coercion and the sensuous motive whereby coercion is to be established) is, as something external, meaningless without the internal, or freedom—and that freedom cannot possibly be severed from coercion. When we consider a criminal action as intending something *specific* which is contrary to the punishment threatened, and to the sensuous motive which the law establishes by that threat, then this specific thing means something sensuous and it will be said that the crime originates from a sensuous impulse. But if the action is regarded as an act of the will, with the implication of the possibility of abstracting from the sensuous motive set up by the law, then it appears as free. Neither view, neither the specific something nor this possibility, can be discarded; the one is flatly bound up with the other, and therefore each can be directly derived from its opposite. But the logic of opinion opines that if something specific, an opposite, is established, we can then actually abstract from the other, the opposite, and dispense with it. Indeed this logic, owing to its sort of principle of contradiction, simply cannot grasp that, with such specific things, the opposite of each is wholly irrelevant in settling what view to take; or that in this abstraction and negative nature one opposite is entirely like the other; and still less can it grasp that the two together, such as freedom contrasted with sense-awareness, and sense-awareness and coercion, are simply nothing real but mere *entia rationis* and creatures of the imagination.

Thus, inasmuch as a science of law is positive because it keeps to opinion and abstractions without substance, it follows that its appeal to experience, or to its criterion of applicability to actuality, or to "healthy common sense" and the common way of looking at things, or even its appeal to philosophy, makes no sense at all.

If we now look more closely at the grounds on which science becomes positive in the manner shown, and in general consider the grounds for appearance and opinion, it is clear that they are in the *form*: what *ideally* is an opposite, one-sided, and has *reality* solely in absolute identity with its opposite, is isolated, put independently, and declared to be real. It is by this form that intuition is directly cancelled, and the whole, dissolved, ceases to be a whole or a reality. Thus this distinction between the positive and the non-positive does not concern the *content*. It is this form which makes it possible not only, as was shown above, for a purely formal abstraction to be fixed and falsely maintained to be truth and reality, but also for a true idea and genuine principle to be misconceived in reference to its limit, and to be laid down apart from the sphere in which it has its truth, so that it loses its truth altogether. The fact that a principle belongs to one sphere is the aspect of its specific character; but in the sphere itself this specific character is present both undifferentiated [from another such character] and also really permeated by the Idea, and this makes it a true principle. In that case the principle is known as the Idea appearing in these specific characters as its shape, but only as the principle of this sphere, and thus its limits and conditions are known. But it is wrested altogether from its truth if in its conditioned character it is made absolute or even extended to cover the nature of other spheres.

The absolute and clear unity of ethical life is absolute and living in virtue of the fact that neither a single sphere nor the subsistence of spheres in general can be fixed—that on the contrary, while ethical life eternally protracts them, at the same time it absolutely collapses and cancels them, and enjoys itself in undeveloped unity and clarity. In relation to the spheres, secure of its own inner life and indivisible, it now reduces one by the other, now passes over wholly into one and destroys the other, and in general withdraws from this movement into absolute rest, in which all are cancelled. On the other hand, sickness and the onset of death are there when one part organizes itself and eludes the dominion of the whole. By this isolation the part affects the whole negatively or even compels it to organize itself for this sphere alone—as, for example, when the vitality of the entrails, in obedience to the whole, develops into individual animals, or the liver makes itself into the ruling organ and forces the whole organism to do its bidding. Thus it may happen that, in the general system of ethical life, the principle and system of civil law, for example, which is concerned with possession and property, becomes wholly absorbed in itself, and in the diffuseness in which it loses itself takes itself to be a totality supposedly inherent, absolute, and unconditioned. The inner negativity of this sphere, even in terms of its content which is the persistently finite, has already been expounded above, and the reflection of the indifference possible in the finite can all the less be taken for an absolute. It is just as impossible to turn the system of acquisition and possession, the wealth of a nation, or a single sphere within this system, be it agriculture, or manufacturing, or trade, into something unconditional.

But a single sphere becomes even more positive if it and its principle so far forget their conditioned character as to encroach on others and subjugate them. Just as the principle of mechanics has intruded into chemistry and natural science, and the principle of chemistry has intruded especially into the latter, so too the philosophy of ethics has at various times been invaded by various principles. Of late, however, in the internal economy of natural law, this external justice (infinity reflected in the persistent finite, and for this reason formal infinity) that constitutes the principle of civil law has secured a special predominance over constitutional and international law. The form of such an inferior relation as the contractual one has forced its way into the absolute majesty of the ethical totality. In the case of the monarchy, for example, the absolute universality of the center and the oneness of the individual therein is understood, now according to a contract of full authorization as a relation between a supreme civil servant to the abstraction of the state, now according to the relation of an ordinary contract as a matter between two specific parties each of whom needs the other, and so as a relation of *quid pro quo*—and by relations of this kind which are wholly in the sphere of the finite, the Idea and the absolute majesty of the ethical totality are destroyed. Similarly, it is inherently a self-contradiction if, in international law, the relation of absolutely independent and free nations (which are ethical totalities) is to be regulated after the model of a civil contract which relates directly to the individuality and dependence of the citizens. So constitutional law too could as such presume to relate directly to the individual, and, as a perfect police, totally permeate his existence and destroy civic freedom (which would be the harshest despotism) in the way in which Fichte* wants to see every action and the whole existence of the individual as an individual supervised, known, and regulated by the universal and the abstraction that are set up in opposition to him. The moral principle could also intrude into the system of absolute ethical life and propose to put itself at the head of public and private law, and international law too. That would be both the greatest weakness and the profoundest despotism, and the complete loss of the Idea of an ethical organization, because the moral principle, like that of civil law, belongs only to the sphere of the finite and the individual.

In science this hardening and isolation of individual principles and their systems, and their encroachment on others, is prevented only by philosophy. The part does not know its own limits but must rather tend to constitute itself a whole and an absolute. Philosophy, however, stands in the Idea of the whole, above the parts; thereby it keeps each part in its limits and also, by the majesty of the Idea itself, prevents the part from burgeoning by subdivision into endless minutiae. In the same way, this limitation and idealization of the various spheres presents itself in reality as the history of the ethical totality. There, in the dimension of time, this totality, secure in its absolute equilibrium, balances between the opposites. At one time, it reminds constitutional law of its specific function by giving a slight preponderance to civil law; at another time, by giving preponder-

---

* [*Grundlage des Naturrechts*, §21.]

ance to the former, it makes breaches and rents in the latter; thus in general it revitalizes each system by for a time inhabiting it more strongly, and reminds all, in their separation, of their impermanence and dependence. What is more, it destroys their uncontrolled growth and their self-organization by at moments confounding all of them at once, presenting them re-absorbed into totality, and letting them go again reborn out of this unity, with the reminder of this dependence and the sense of their weakness if they wanted to be on their own.

This character of the positivity of legal science affects the form whereby one sphere isolates itself and sets itself up as absolute. By such a course, religion and whatever else (and indeed any philosophy) can become perverted and corrupted. But we must study positivity also from the material side. For although both (what we have earlier called positive, and what we are now studying as material) belong to the sphere of the particular, we earlier dealt with the external linking of the form of universality with particularity and specification, while now we are dealing with the particular as such.

And in this context we must above all guard against formalism in respect of everything that, in terms of its matter, can be posited as positive. For formalism disrupts perception and its identity of the universal and the particular, and places the abstractions of universal and particular in opposition, while counting anything it can exclude from this emptiness, but subsume under the abstraction of particularity, as something positive. It does not consider that by this opposition [of particular to universal] the universal becomes positive just as much as the particular. For, as was shown above, it becomes positive through the form of opposition in which it is present in that abstraction. The real, however, is a sheer identity of the universal and the particular; therefore, that abstraction and positing of one of the opposites that arise from this abstraction, the positing of the universal as inherently self-subsistent, cannot take place. In general, if formal thinking is logical, it must be altogether devoid of content if it conceives the particular as positive. In the pure reason of formal thinking, every multiplicity and distinguishability must altogether disappear, and it is quite impossible to see how even the scantiest multiplicity of rubrics and headings could be obtained. Indeed, those who conceive the nature of the organism to be the abstraction of some vital force must, strictly speaking, conceive of the limbs and the brain and the heart and the viscera as something particular, positive, and accidental, and leave them out.

Like everything living, ethical life is a sheer identity of universal and particular, and for that reason is an individuality and a shape. It carries in itself particularity, necessity, relation (i.e., relative identity), but these are identified with and assimilated to it, so that it is free in this identity. And this ethical life, which reflection may consider to be particularity, is not something positive, or opposed to the living individual which is thereby tied to chance and necessity, but is alive. This side is its inorganic nature, though it has attached that side organically to itself in shape and individuality. Thus, to mention the most common thing, the specific climate of a people— and its epoch in the development of the race—belong to necessity. And of the far-flung chain of necessity, only one link covers this people's present period; this link can be understood, in one respect, in terms of geography, and, in another, of history. But the individuality of ethical life has organized itself into this link, and the specific character of this link depends not on this individuality but on necessity. For the ethical vitality of the people lies precisely in the fact that the people has a shape in which a specific character is present—though not as something positive (in our use of this word so far) but as something absolutely united with universality and animated by it. And this aspect is very important also, partly in order to recognize how philosophy learns to honor necessity; partly because this aspect is a whole, and only a narrow view sees merely the individual detail and rejects it as accidental; and partly also because this aspect cancels the view of the individual and accidental by showing that it does not inherently hinder life, but that life, on the contrary, by letting the individual and accidental persist as they are of necessity, removes them from this necessity and permeates and vitalizes them. The element of water to which part of the animal kingdom organically adapts itself, and the element of air, to which another part does, are not something dead or positive because they are single elements, one for the fish and the other for the bird. Neither is *this* form, in which ethical life is organized in *this* climate and *this* period of a particular or universal culture, something positive *there*. Just as the totality of life is fully as present in the nature of the polyp as in that of the nightingale and the lion, so the world-spirit, in every one of its shapes, has enjoyed its self-awareness, weaker or more developed but always absolute; it has enjoyed itself and its own essence in every nation under every system of laws and customs.

This stage is thus justified externally; this external aspect belongs to necessity as such. For even in this abstraction of necessity, singularity is again simply cancelled by the Idea. This singularity of the stage of polyp and nightingale and lion is an element in a whole, and in this connection with the whole it is respected. Over the single stages there floats the idea of totality which, however, is mirrored back by its whole scattered image, and sees and recognizes itself therein. This totality of the widespread image is the justification of the single as an existent. It is therefore the *formal* standpoint which gives the form of particularity to an individuality and cancels the life in which particularity is real; it is the *empirical* standpoint, on the other hand, which demands a higher stage where the reality of a specific stage is laid down. That higher stage, even in its developed reality, is empirically just as much present [as the lower one]; the higher development of the life of the plant is present in the polyp, the polyp's higher development in the insect, etc. Only empirical unreason proposes to discern in the polyp the empirical manifestation of the higher stage of the insect. A polyp, assuming it were not a polyp, still is nothing but this specific dead bit of matter, empirically related to me—dead matter because I take it for an empty possibility of being something else, and this emptiness is death. If it is a question of the higher manifestation, with absolutely no empirical relation, that manifestation can be found; for, in accordance with absolute necessity, it must be there.

Thus the feudal system, for example, may well appear as something entirely positive. But in the first place, from the aspect of necessity, it is not something absolute and single; it exists wholly in the totality of necessity. But inwardly, in face of life itself, the question whether the feudal system is positive depends entirely on whether the nation has truly organized itself within that system as an individuality, whether it completely fills the shape of this system and vitally permeates it—whether the law of these relations is *ethos*. Thus if, for example, the genius of a people is in general on a lower level and weaker, and the weakness of ethical life is at its most stubborn in barbarism and in a formal culture; if the nation has allowed itself to be conquered by another and has had to lose its independence (i.e., if it has preferred misfortune, and the disgrace of loss of independence, to battle and death); if it has sunk so crudely into the reality of animal life that it does not even rise to formal ideality, to the abstraction of a universal, and thus in determining relationships for physical necessities cannot bear the relation of law but only of personality; or, equally, if the reality of the universal and of law has lost all conviction and truth, and the nation cannot feel and enjoy the image of divinity in its own being, but must put that image outside itself and must make do instead with a dim feeling, or even the painful feeling of vast distance and lofty eminence: if all this occurs, then the feudal system and serfdom have absolute truth, and this relationship is the one possible form of ethical life and is therefore the necessary and just and ethical form.

This individuality of the whole, and the specific character of a nation, then do indeed allow us to understand the whole system into which the absolute totality organizes itself. We can understand how all parts of the constitution and the laws, all specific details of ethical relationships, are entirely determined by the whole and form a structure in which no joint and no ornament has been independently present *a priori*, but each element has been brought about by the whole and is subservient to it. In this sense Montesquieu based his immortal work on the view of the individuality and character of nations, and while he did not rise to the height of the most living Idea, he yet did not merely deduce individual institutions and laws from so-called reason, nor merely abstract them from experience to raise them thereafter to some universal. On the contrary, he comprehended both the higher relationships of constitutional law and the lower specifications of civil relationships down to wills, marriage laws, etc., entirely from the character of the whole and its individuality. And those empirical theorists who imagine that they understand the accidents of their political and legal systems through reason, or that they have derived these systems from common-sense itself or even from common experience, have been shown by Montesquieu in a way comprehensible to them that reason and common-sense and experience, from which specific laws arise, are not reason and common-sense *a priori* or experience *a priori*, which would be absolutely universal. He has shown that these systems are wholly and solely the living individuality of a nation, an individuality whose highest specifications are to be comprehended once again from a more universal necessity.

It has been shown above in reference to science that each individual sphere can be fixed and that science thereby can become positive; and the same claim must be made in reference to the ethical individual or the nation. For in accordance with necessity, the totality must present itself in the individual and the nation as the persistence of the dispersed characteristics; and the single link in the chain, within which the individual and the nation are set in the present, must pass on and give place to another. Since the individual grows in this way and one sphere emerges more strongly, while another recedes, the parts organized in the latter find themselves ejected and dead. This division, in which some things mature towards new life while others, which have become settled at the stage of one specific feature, remain behind and see life flow away from them, is possible only because the specific feature of one stage has become fixed and made formally absolute. The form of law which is given to the specific *ethos*, and which is universality or the negative absolute of identity, lends to the *ethos* the appearance of something inherently [necessary]. If the mass of a nation is large, so too is that part of it which is organized in the specific feature of that stage; and the law's consciousness of this large part greatly outweighs the law's unconsciousness of the newly emerging life. When *ethos* and law were one, the specific feature was not anything positive. But if the whole does not advance in step with the growth of the individual, law and *ethos* separate; the living unity binding the members together is weakened and there is no longer any absolute cohesion and necessity in the present life of the whole. At this stage, therefore, the individual cannot be understood on his own, since his specific character lacks the life which explains it and makes it intelligible; and since the new *ethos* now also begins to shape itself into laws, an inner contradiction of laws amongst themselves is simply bound to arise. In the foregoing, history is only one side of the picture, and what is necessary is also free, while here, by contrast, necessity is no longer at one with freedom and thus falls prey entirely to pure history. If something has no true ground in the present, its ground lies in a past; and so we must look for a time in which the specific feature, fixed in law but now dead, was a living *ethos* and in harmony with the rest of the laws. But beyond precisely this aim to know, the effect of a purely historical explanation of laws and institutions cannot go. It would exceed its function and truth if it were used to justify, for the present time, the law which had truth only in a life that is past. On the contrary, this historical knowledge of the law, which can exhibit the ground of the law only in lost customs and a life that is dead, proves precisely that now in the living present the law lacks understanding and meaning, even though it still may have power and force on the strength of the form of law, owing to the fact that parts of the whole are still in its interest and survive because of it.

But to distinguish properly what is dead and without truth from what is still living, we must recall a distinction which can elude a formal insight and which must prevent us from taking what is inherently negative for the living law, and the rule of inherently negative laws for the life of the organization. For laws which withdraw specific features and parts from the supremacy of the whole, which preclude the law from ruling over them, and which exempt the individual from the universal, are inherently negative and are the signs of approaching death—a death which becomes ever more menacing to life as these negatives and withdrawals increase in number, and as these laws tending towards this disintegration get the upper hand of the true laws constituting the unity of the whole. Therefore, among the positive and the dead there must not merely be counted what belongs entirely to a past and what no longer has any living present and possesses only an unintelligent and, for lack of an inner meaning, shameless power; but that too which establishes the negative (i.e., the disintegration and severance from the ethical whole) is devoid of genuinely positive truth. The former is the history of a past life, the latter the definite representation of present death.

Thus, in a disintegrated nation such as the German, the laws may of course appear to have truth, provided we do not distinguish between whether they are laws of the negative and of separation, or laws of the truly positive and of unity. When laws organizing a whole have meaning solely for a past, and relate to a shape and an individuality discarded long ago as a dead husk; when they are no longer interested in any but parts of the whole, and therefore establish no living relation to the whole but confront it as a foreign power and rule; when those things which express a living bond and inner unity are no longer appropriate in the slightest as means to their ends, and the means therefore have neither intelligibility nor truth (because the truth of a means lies in its adequacy to the end); when this inmost lack of truth of the whole results after all in there being little truth in the science of philosophy in general, in ethical life, and in religion too—then indeed disintegraion is confirmed and stabilized; it settles in a system of the negative and so puts on the formal semblance of knowledge, and of laws whose inner essence is nothingness. If the knowledge and science of such a people asserts that reason comprehends and knows nothing and consists only in empty freedom (i.e., in a flight, in nothingness and its appearance), then the content and essence of the negative legislation is that there is no law, no unity, no whole. The former untruth is the one that is untrue unknowingly and innocently; but this second untruth is the one that entrenches itself by arrogating form to itself.

Thus it is not philosophy which takes the particular for something positive, just because it is a particular. On the contrary, philosophy does so only if the particular has won independence as a single part outside the absolute cohesion of the whole. The absolute totality restricts itself as necessity in each of its spheres, produces itself out of them as a totality, and recapitulates there the preceding spheres just as it anticipates the succeeding ones. But one of these is the greatest power, in whose color and character the totality appears, yet without being in any way restrictive for life any more than water is for the fish or air for the bird. At the same time it is necessary for individuality to advance through metamorphoses, and for all that belongs to the dominant stage to weaken and die, so that all stages of necessity appear as such stages in this individuality. But the misfortune of the period of transition (i.e., that this strengthening of the new formation has not yet cleansed itself absolutely of the past) is where the positive resides. And although nature, within a specific form, advances with a uniform (not mechanically uniform, but uniformly accelerated) movement, it still enjoys a new form which it acquires. As nature enters that form, so it remains in it, just as a shell starts suddenly towards its zenith and then rests for a moment in it;* metal, when heated, does not turn soft like wax, but all at once becomes liquid and remains so—for this phenomenon is the transition into the absolute opposite and so is infinite, and this emergence of the opposite out of infinity or out of its nothingness is a leap. The shape, in its new-born strength, at first exists for itself alone, before it becomes conscious of its relation to an other. Just so, the growing individuality has both the delight of the leap in entering a new form and also an enduring pleasure in its new form, until it gradually opens up to the negative, and in its decline too it is sudden and brittle.

Now the philosophy of ethics teaches us to comprehend this necessity, and to know the connection of its content and the content's specific character as absolutely bound up with the spirit, and as its living body; it opposes itself to the formalism which regards as contingent and dead what it can subsume under the concept of particularity. At the same time, this philosophy recognizes that this vitality of individuality as such, whatever its shape, is a formal vitality. For the restrictedness of what belongs to necessity, even if it be absolutely absorbed into indifference, is only a part of necessity, not absolute total necessity itself, and so it is always an incongruity between absolute spirit and its shape. But it cannot attain this absolute shape by escaping into the shapelessness of cosmopolitanism, still less into the void of the Rights of Man, or the like void of a league of nations or a world republic. These are abstractions and formalisms filled with exactly the opposite of

---

* [Prior to Newton it was believed that a projectile came momentarily to rest at the upward point of its trajectory before beginning its downward flight.]

ethical vitality and which in their essence are protestants against individuality and are revolutionary, while philosophy must descry the most beautiful shape befitting the high Idea of absolute ethical life. Since the absolute Idea is in itself absolute intuition, its construction immediately determines also the purest and freest individuality in which spirit intuits and beholds itself with perfect objectivity in its shape, and, without returning into itself out of intuition, immediately recognizes itself in intuition itself, and by that very recognition is absolute spirit and perfect ethical life. At the same time, in the manner presented above, this life fends off involvement with the negative—for (since what we have so far called positive has in the event turned out to be the negative considered in itself) it confronts the negative as objective and fate, and by consciously conceding to the negative a power and a realm, at the sacrifice of a part of itself, it maintains its own life purified of the negative.

Index ❦

$3.95

G. W. F. HEGEL
NATURAL LAW

Translated by **T. M. Knox**
Introduction by **H. B. Acton**

"Acton's introduction should bring the NATURAL LAW within the grasp of the beginning student of Hegel while providing a level of scholarship and insight to interest the mature philosopher ..."
— **John R. Silber**

This long-awaited English translation of NATURAL LAW provides a valuable insight into Hegel's political thought and its subsequent impact on Karl Marx.

The Introduction by H. B. Acton offers a useful commentary on the historical and philosophical background of the NATURAL LAW together with an exposition and analysis of many of its central issues. Acton traces Hegel's early philosophical development and then examines Hegel's treatment of natural law (within the context of "pure" as opposed to "scientific" empiricism) and his struggle with the formalism of Kant's theory of morality. He concludes with a detailed discussion of the relation of the ethical life and the role of law in civil society, including Hegel's view of history.

Sir Malcolm Knox is Professor Emeritus of the University of St. Andrews, Scotland.

A volume in WORKS IN CONTINENTAL PHILOSOPHY, edited by John R. Silber.

Pennsylvania Paperback 83
Jacket Design By: Tom Jackson
University of Pennsylvania Press